Heroes of the
Round Table

Heroes
- of the -
Round
Table

Mike Dixon-Kennedy

BLANDFORD

For Gill, my Guinevere;
and Christopher, Charlotte, Thomas and Rebecca,
my very own Knights of the Round Table

A BLANDFORD BOOK

First published in the UK 1997 by Blandford

A Cassell Imprint

Cassell Plc, Wellington House,
125 Strand, London WC2R 0BB

Copyright © Mike Dixon-Kennedy

Distributed in the United States by Sterling Publishing Co., Inc.,
387 Park Avenue South, New York, NY 10016–8810

**A Cataloguing-in-Publication Data entry for this title
is available from the British Library**

ISBN 0–7137–2619–9

Designed and typeset by Ben Cracknell Studios

Printed and bound by Colorcraft, Hong Kong.

Contents

Preface

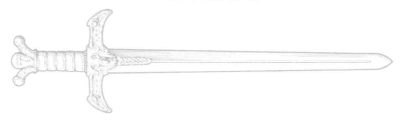

WHEN I WAS FIRST ASKED to consider writing a book about the heroes of the Round Table I had very definite ideas of my own about the Round Table itself. However, during my research, I have had those ideas altered. Previously I had thought of the Round Table as purely fictional; now I am not so sure. I now believe that there is some historical substance to the many, many stories that surround that enigmatic king, his knights and the Round Table just as there is to the figure of King Arthur himself.

I found myself taken on a journey of discovery, or perhaps rediscovery, a journey that started long before King Arthur had even been born. To appreciate the need for heroes such as Arthur and his knights, I thought it necessary to look into the history of the Celtic people themselves, a history that is both as fascinating as the legends I was researching and also essential to our understanding of the circumstances the Celts found themselves in during the period when Arthur came to the fore. For that sole reason, Part One of the book gives a history of the Celts, from their origins in central Europe, through the Roman oppression, to the Middle Ages, when the romanticists went to work on Arthur and turned him into the character so well known today.

The journey I undertook not only advanced my own personal understanding of the Celtic peoples but also altered my perception of both the Round Table, placing it on a historical footing, and King Arthur himself. Though I will always fervently believe that once, many centuries ago, King Arthur did indeed walk upon English soil to lead his forces into battle against overwhelming odds, I can no longer consider him with as much reverence as I did, for upon closer study of the knights he chose to surround himself with, he appears an almost pathetic figure, who was easily led, misled, betrayed, teased, deceived, tricked and eventually defeated.

None of this is intended to put King Arthur down, for he is still the classic example of a culture-hero *par excellence*. However, it is intended to make you think, as it has made me think, about just what was going through the minds of those ancient writers who first recorded the legends for our subsequent enjoyment. Maybe his weak character had something to do with the personal likes and dislikes of the writers. Or perhaps it has some foundation in history. Whatever the reason, I hope that by referring to King Arthur in this way, and by studying not just the king but those of his entourage who would undoubtedly have guided, or misguided, him, I will enable you to reach your own conclusions as to why King Arthur, having risen to such prominence, allowed so many of his court to take unfair advantage of him, particularly those closest to him. The truth is possibly quite simple: King Arthur never asked to be king; that position was forced upon him and he may simply have been too nice a man for the role.

As with the writing of any book, there are people who deserve my unreserved thanks. *Heroes of the Round Table* would never have seen the light of day if it had not been for Stuart Booth at Cassell, who suggested the book to me in the first place and then helped me to structure and organize it. Credit must also be given to Chris Down for the marvellous colour plates that portray the various heroes of the Round Table so vividly, for they bring the characters I have written about to life in a way that words alone cannot express. Last, but by no means least, my wife, Gill, and my four children, who once again have my undying admiration for their patience and tolerance. Without the love and support of my wife I would not have had the time to apply myself to the task of writing the book, and without the cooperation of my children there would never have been enough peace in our busy house for me to concentrate.

Mike Dixon-Kennedy
Cornwall, England.

Introduction

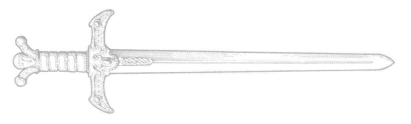

EVERYBODY HAS THEIR OWN IDEAS about what makes a hero. To a young child it might be the fireman who has just rescued a pet cat from the branches of a tall tree. To an adult it might be an individual who has overcome some disability, or behaved selflessly in dangerous circumstances, or excelled on the sports field – or, indeed, any one of a hundred other things. In its dictionary definition, the term simply refers to someone distinguished by exceptional courage or nobility, and the latter is of prime importance in the context of this book, for many of the heroes appear to have gained their 'heroic' status simply by means of their birthright. At first glance, the thesaurus merely confuses the picture, as this lists a whole host of words that can equally be applied to a hero: for example, celebrity, champion, conqueror, exemplar, great man, heart-throb, protagonist, star, super-star, victor. But, perhaps this list illustrates the type of hero portrayed here better than would at first appear. We have the celebrity in Merlin, the champion in Lancelot (though he equally well exhibits attributes that could be applied to any of these words), the conqueror in Gareth, the exemplar in Galahad, the great man in Arthur, the heart-throb in Lancelot, the protagonist in Mordred and in Kay, the star and super-star in just about all of them in different ways, and the victor, albeit regrettably, in Mordred. All the Knights of the Round Table exhibit at least one of the attributes from the list, depending on which source is consulted. I have here simply chosen the words that I think best sum up each character. You, of course, might prefer different ones, and therein lies the main problem with the depiction of a hero – we all have our own ideas and ideals.

This difficulty is what has determined my approach to the book. I have decided not to try to connect any particular attribute to any of the characters. Instead, I have investigated the status of the Celtic people over the centuries prior to the birth, either actual or poetic, of King Arthur and, having completed my researches, have retold the stories of those from among the coterie of King Arthur who best display one or more of the heroic traits given in the thesaurus list. Additionally, I have looked for not just individuals with these traits but whole characterizations that run consistently throughout the vast body of Arthurian literature.

When considering the structure of the book I looked at various different options. In the end, I decided it was important to start with a brief background history of the Celts, because this was instrumental in determining the way that medieval writers fashioned the stories surrounding King Arthur and, therefore, the characters of the Knights of the Round Table. If I had omitted the history of the Celts and waded straight into the characters and their stories, a vital element would have been missing: the reasons the Celts felt the need to elevate a person from the ranks to kingship, and to characterize the knights as they did (though, of course, many of these characters undoubtedly owe their origins not to the fifth- and sixth-century Celts, but to the poetic minds of the medieval writers who took the earlier material and sculpted it into the form known and loved today).

The hardest single task I had while writing the book was to decide on just who should be profiled in depth. I would have loved to go to the same lengths on many other characters, but such are the constraints of a book of this nature that I have had to be selective. I hope that I have managed to pick a representative cross-section of the hero types that are to be found within the brotherhood of the Round Table. However, to counteract the omission of the characters from the main profiles, I have added a chapter in Part One that was not originally envisaged, and in it I have briefly outlined the majority of the other characters who might have, at one time or another, had a seat at the Round Table (see pages 38–561).

Purists might argue about some of my choices, but my main concern was to make this book accessible to one and all. I have tried to detail the origins of each character, showing how he developed into the Arthurian knight we know today. Deliberately omitted are the scholarly arguments that cloud much of the study of Arthurian myth, legend and literature. Such argument belongs in learned tomes that aim to deconstruct the legends and take them back to their roots. Instead, I have concentrated on the best known characterizations and shown how these characters fit within the coterie that surrounded Arthur and their effect on his kingship.

The single most remarkable thing that all this goes to show is that none of the knights actually helped King Arthur to any great extent. Sure enough, they all came to the Round Table with the best intentions and started out well, but it wasn't too long after the foundation of the order of the Knights of the Round Table that the first dissenting voice was raised against king and country.

The study of each individual illustrates only the role that that particular person played, but to read them all will give you a clear picture of the problems that King

Arthur had to face, the dissent he had to endure, the treachery he chose to ignore, the schemes, plots and plans of a few, and the wider implications of each. Some knights abided by their codes of chivalry with almost religious fervour, while others used their position to enhance their own status, as if being a Knight of the Round Table were not enough in itself. The bottom line is that the medieval writers responsible for the records of King Arthur and his knights looked at the attributes and characteristics of their fellow men, and then applied them to the stories they were relating. There is no way of telling how accurate these characterizations were, but many of them hold as true today as they did then. Indeed, I know many people who have qualities comparable with those of the Knights of the Round Table. A good friend would make a perfect Sir Kay, for example, and I am sure that you too will be able to see similarities in many of your acquaintances.

The book's structure allows you to use it in more than one way. Ultimately, it should enable you to draw your own conclusions about the Knights of the Round Table: why they acted in the way they did, why King Arthur ever chose them to join the order in the first place and what role they played in either the support or the destruction of the kingdom. However, not everyone will want to go to these lengths and many will probably delve straight into the chapters on those characters they are most interested in. Therefore, I have made it possible to read each profile by itself; the story is complete. Historians will be interested in the background and they have been catered for. I would, however, recommend that Part One be read at least once by everybody, for not to do so would be to omit the essence that actually gave life to many of the characters. In Part One I have looked not just at the origins of the Celtic people but also at how they dispersed through Europe and ended up in Wales, England and Ireland. From those origins I have then continued their history through the oppression of the Roman and Anglo-Saxon invasions, and discussed why the Celts might have felt the need for a super-hero the likes of whom had never been seen before — and has yet to be seen again. Additionally, I have tried not to clutter the text with academic theories, but have instead used extensive endnotes, which can be read by those who wish to glean just a little more information and ignored by those who are simply interested in the stories themselves.

It is obviously extremely hard structuring a book of this nature to appeal to everyone, but I have tried to make the text open and accessible, yet authoritative and complete. Hopefully you will find that it fills a gap in your Arthurian bookshelf, furthering your enjoyment of the subject and stimulating you to continue your researches. This interest is necessary to increase our understanding of our origins and just what our ancestors had to endure. With a distinct lack of contemporary early English historical records (those that do exist are mostly fanciful), we have to rely on legendary and mythological concepts to determine our roots. King Arthur may never have been a king, but his importance is indicative of the times he lived in and the importance our ancestors placed on him and his entourage.

PART ONE

Background History

Who Were the Celts?

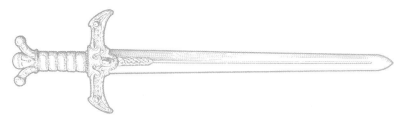

IN ORDER TO UNDERSTAND the times during which the main body of Arthurian literature was written it is first essential to spend a short time relating a brief history of the Celtic people, to show how their many transitions and migrations, along with their eventual suppression and conquest, shaped the legends of King Arthur and the Knights of the Round Table.

Celtic history is, to say the very least, obscure. It is hard to study the period prior to written accounts, and archaeological sources can only sketch the outlines. We have to use common sense and a degree of intuition to fill in the gaps. In the following history, the story of the Celts unfolds from their origins to their suppression at the hands of the Romans and the Anglo-Saxons. Even though today the Celts have all but vanished from the face of the earth, they were once one of the most magnificent of all early civilizations, and we can only wonder what would have happened had the Romans decided to leave England alone.

The earliest references to the Celts appear in the chronicles of classical authors about 500 years before the birth of Christ and indicate that they obviously occupied a position of great strength and influence in the then unknown areas of middle Europe. These mysterious people, possibly even considered legendary at that time, were referred to as Hyperboreans[1] by the Greeks. The term Celt (Keltoi in Greek) was first used *c*.500 BC by the geographer Hecataeus of Miletus (*c*. 550–476 BC) who refers to 'Nyrax, a Celtic city' and to 'Massalia [Marseilles], a city of Liguria in the land of the Celts'.[2] Classical legend accounts for the naming of the Celts through Celtina, the daughter of Britanus, who had a son by Heracles named Celtus who became the progenitor of the Celtic people.

Herodotus (*c*. 485–425 BC), writing approximately 50 years later, records that the Celts dwelt 'beyond the Pillars of Hercules' (i.e. in Spain) and states that the

River Danube rose in their country. All this is consistent with current thinking, which says that the Celts originated *c.*1200 BC in central Europe in the basin of the upper Danube, the Alps and parts of France and southern Germany. Between the ninth and fifth centuries BC the Celts developed a transitional culture between the Bronze and Iron Ages that subsequently became known as the Halstatt culture, from the results of excavations carried out in 1846 in the saltmines at Halstatt, southwest of Salzburg. Here a pre-Roman necropolis, or burial site, was uncovered containing relics that were believed to date from *c.*750 to *c.*400 BC. These relics were the first true indicators of a once magnificent society with a very high standard of civilization, and considerable commercial acumen. Amber from the Baltic, glass from Phoenicia and Oriental gold leaf were all discovered at Halstatt, artefacts that were to rewrite much of the early history of Europe. For the first time arms from the period were also found, notably iron swords whose hilts and sheaths were richly embellished with gold, ivory and amber. This was no foundling society, but rather one that had developed over several hundred years.

Around the sixth century BC they spread into Spain and Portugal, where they intermarried with the indigenous Iberian peoples and were known as the Celtiberi – literally 'Iberian Celts'. Over the following 300 years the Celts fanned out from their heartland, most notably sacking Rome in 390 BC, the date of the battle being recorded as 18 July, as well as settling in Greece and the Balkans, though they never established a united empire, probably because theirs was a tribal society, not lending itself readily to union.

It was also about this time that they travelled up through France, crossed the English Channel and arrived in Britain *c.*400 BC, coming in two waves. The first to arrive were the Goidelic Celts,[3] of whom traces may still be seen in the Gaels of Ireland and the Highlands, as well as on the Isle of Man. They were followed by the Brythonic Celts, or Bretons, who were closely allied in descent and culture to the Gauls of France, and of whom traces may still be found in the Welsh, Cornish, Breton and Gaulish peoples. It is these later Celts who are of primary interest to the English, as the Goidelic Celts took an altogether different route, landing first in Ireland, which they quickly occupied, before moving northwards to cross from Ireland into Scotland. They never travelled up through France, but instead sailed from the Iberian peninsula and landed in southern Ireland. Irish mythology clearly records this, as it refers to the first Celtic invaders as the Sons of Míl Éspáine – the sons of Míl of Spain.[4]

Aristotle (384–322 BC) clearly had knowledge of the Celts. He referred to them as living 'beyond Spain', and knew that they had sacked and captured Rome. He also states that they set great store by warlike power, and that they were a fearsome warrior people. It is not surprising, therefore, that when they arrived in Ireland and Britain they met with little resistance from the pastoral peoples living there.

Further evidence of the ordered society of the Celts comes from the writings of Hellanicus of Lesbos (*c.* fifth century BC), who clearly states that the Celts practised

This page:
Sixth- or seventh-century bronze Pennanular brooch. (British Museum.)

Opposite:
Gündestrup Cauldron: silver internal panel depicting warriors going into battle, preceded by a ram-horned snake. (Nationalmuseet, Denmark.)

a highly organized form of justice and fervently believed in righteousness. Ephorus (*c.*350 BC) states that the Celts living in Greece had adopted the same rites and customs as the Greeks and were on the friendliest of terms with their hosts. Plato (*c.*428–*c.*348 BC), however, begs to differ, for in his *Laws* he classes the Celts as a barbarian and drunken people, capable of the most despicable acts of barbarity, particularly during their sack of Delphi in 273 BC.

It is from these scattered references that the early history of the Celts must be reconstructed, along with the notable efforts of those archaeologists who excavated the remarkable sites of Halstatt and La Tène. This latter, a settlement at the northeastern end of Lake Neuchâtel, Switzerland, which was excavated in 1858, revealed artefacts that undoubtedly represented the culminating period of Gaulish civilization and date from around the third century BC. The fragmentary reconstruction of early Celtic history is a necessary evil as no contemporary early Celtic chronicles have survived, if indeed any were ever compiled. Of their architecture we know very little, for they chose to build from wood, and of their culture we have only a few fragmentary artefacts, though some of these are truly astounding, particularly the wondrous Gündestrup Cauldron, a ceremonial vessel dating from the first or second century BC that was discovered in a peat bog in Vesthimmerland in north Jutland, Denmark, in 1891. Perhaps the most recognizable relic of the Celtic culture that has been passed down into modern day are their place-names, which, though now long altered, are uniquely Celtic and serve to remind us of the days in which the Celtic people were dominant within Europe and, who knows,

possibly beyond, for certain Celtic influences seem to surface in the Slavonic cultures of Asia.

When we talk about the Celtic people it is very important to remember that there has never been a single, homogeneous Celtic race. However, as the results of numerous archaeological excavations seem to suggest, they shared common features and are best described as tall, fair-haired – red rather than the Germanic blond – warlike and well organized. From their heartland somewhere within the Danube basin, the Celts spread outwards, occupying new lands not only by conquest but also by peaceful infiltration and integration. By whichever method they used to move into a new domain, they did not seek to exterminate the original inhabitants, but rather to impose on them their customs and traditions, their language and their arts, at the same time learning much along the way. Thus each time the Celts moved into a new area, they actually formed a new subrace, for not only would they occupy and thus rule, but they would also intermarry, their offspring being the core of any new race. However, it was exactly this social structure that was ultimately to be the downfall of the Celtic people of Europe. In many respects, the Celts of Europe were one of the most attractive and promising of all ancient cultures, but they suffered from the single inability to discard their tribal origins and form a coherent nation. If they had, then who can tell what Europe would have been like today?

Even though we can now, as already mentioned, quite accurately determine that the Celts originated *c.*1200 BC, the first 700 years of their history, and perhaps the most interesting phase of Celtic development, will always remain a mystery, for of

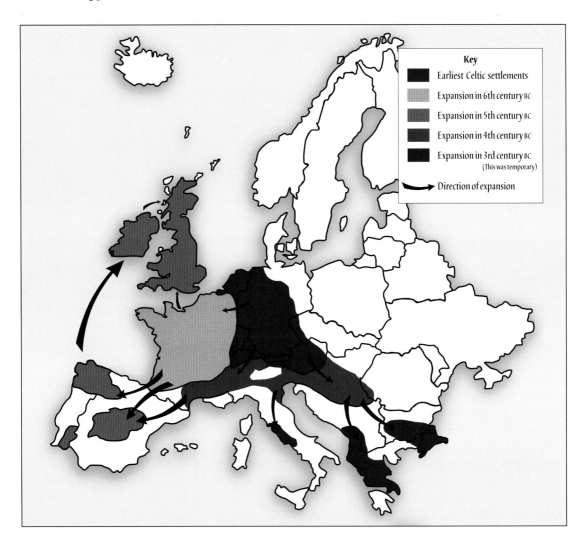

Map showing Celtic expansion through the centuries.

that period nothing is recorded. The only evidence we have of the movements of the Celts comes from the discovery of artefacts that are Celtic, and these are few and far between. However, from the fifth century BC onwards, things become a little easier, for here we have the reports of early chroniclers and can add small snippets of information gleaned from excavations.

Some time between 600 BC and 500 BC the Celts took Spain from the Carthaginians.[5] Around 400 BC they moved into northern Italy and took on the might of the Etruscans – no mean feat, for the Etruscans, the earliest known Italian civilization, were just as warlike as the Celts. However, prevail they did and in 390 BC, under the leadership of a Gaulish Celt by the name of Brennos, they succeeded in sacking and taking Rome. Having established a firm foothold, they settled in large numbers in the area that was later to become known as Cisalpine Gaul where many place-names, such as Virodunum (Verduno), Addua (Adda) and Mediolanum (Milan), to this day testify to their occupation of the region.

From this established Mediterranean stronghold the Celts moved to the east and towards the end of the fourth century BC overran that area that today covers the former Yugoslavia and thus subjugated the Illyrians. However, prior to this the Celts had moved slightly further east and southwards, for they had already settled in Greece and were on the friendliest of terms with their Greek hosts. Indeed, so good was their relationship that all three wars – in Spain, in Italy, and in the Balkans – were undertaken with the help of the Greeks. But theirs was not help simply for the sake of helping friends, for the Greeks had definite trading aspirations that they saw the Celts as capable of helping them achieve.

By their occupation of Spain the Celts had opened up to the Greeks the tin and silver trades that had previously been managed by the Carthaginians. They also opened up the overland trading route across France to Britain and secured the port of Marseilles, which had been deliberately founded by the Phocaeans[6] to service this route, for use by the Greeks. Greeks and Celts also allied against both the Persians and the Phoenicians, an alliance that was so strong that it actually prevented the Carthaginians from lending their support to the Persians, even though by doing so they could have overcome their common enemy. Such was the fear of the Celts who fought so ferociously that sight of just one was alleged to turn the blood cold and make brave men flee for their very lives. The alliance of the Greeks and the Celts must surely have been a contributory factor to the longevity of the classical Greek world, contributing also to the ultimate survival of many of the artefacts and wonders from that great culture, which make it the most easily studied of all ancient cultures.

The Celts furthered their alliance with the Greeks under Alexander the Great. During the fourth century BC Macedon was attacked and all but annihilated by Illyrians and Thracians. King Amyntas II was defeated and driven into exile, while his son Perdiccas II was killed in battle (c.367 or 359 BC). Philip (382–336 BC), the youngest son of Amyntas II, ascended to the throne and set about restoring the kingdom of Macedon with the help of the Celts. This alliance was probably placed on a more formal footing after the death of Philip, when the throne of Macedon passed to his son Alexander (356–323 BC), who is better known as Alexander the Great. While preparing to undertake the conquest of Asia in 334 BC, Alexander made a prudent pact with the Ionian Celts, thus protecting his Macedonian kingdom from attack during his absence, an episode that is recorded by Ptolemy I Soter (d. 283 BC).

The Celtic Invasion of Britain

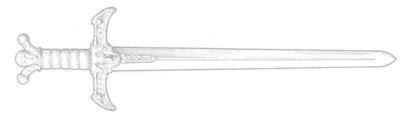

WITH MUCH OF EUROPE now under their influence, or even control, the Celts next made the logical move of travelling across the English Channel to arrive in England some time around 400 BC. The Celts who occupied England and then spread out through the country were Brythonic Celts, for the Goidelic Celts of Ireland and later Scotland, sailed from Spain to land in Ireland, and, except perhaps for exploratory raids made on the western fringes of England and Wales, never settled in either country.

When the Celts arrived they would have found a society that appears to have been fairly similar to their own, apart from the fact that the Britons were totally pastoral and thus easily subjugated. However, there is no evidence to support the theory that the Celts did indeed conquer England. Rather, they appear to have landed, been welcomed warmly and set about their conquest by peaceful means. They intermarried, adopted (and later adapted) the island religion, and slowly assimilated the ancient Britons within their own society. No one can accurately say how many years all of this took, but it seems likely that within 100 years of the Celts first landing, England was a Celtic land.

The most major change that the Celts brought with them was to the native religion of England and Wales. Modern thinking holds that the Druids of England and Wales, and to a lesser extent Scotland and Ireland, were markedly different from their Continental counterparts. Whereas the Druids of the Continent worshipped in natural sites – groves, woods, thickets, etc. – the British Druids worshipped within the multitude of Neolithic stone circles that may still be seen scattered over the British landscape, and indeed much farther afield, thus suggesting that the early Celtic priesthood of Continental Europe had already applied the logic they were about to apply in Britain.

Stonehenge. Legend says that this famous monument originated in Africa and found its way to Salisbury Plain by way of Ireland and Merlin's Magic. Archaeology tells us otherwise. (Michael J. Stead.)

The stone circles, which predate any history that can be accurately recorded, had been long in use as religious centres by the so-called Megalithic[1] people. Why, then, should the Celts not also adopt this usage, for that way they could be seen to be wanting not to obliterate current beliefs, but to adapt their own religious life to that of the native inhabitants.

The two most prominent stone circles that the invading Celts would have found in use were Avebury and Stonehenge, both of which are situated in a small region of Wiltshire that is rich in ancient artefacts and monuments. Stonehenge, possibly the best known Neolithic monument in the world, started life, archaeological evidence tells us, some time around 2800 BC as a ditch and bank along with the so-called 'heel stone'. Some 800 years later the monument was added to when blue-stone pillars, possibly originating in the Preseli Hills in Wales, were brought to the site and erected, their passage to the site probably meaning that they were floated up the River Avon. These pillars formed what is today the inner horseshoe of the ring. Finally, another 500 years later, sarsen trilithons were erected to complete the structure. The purpose of Stonehenge has always been, and probably always will be, an enigma, but the alignment of certain stones with the rising sun at the summer and winter solstices must surely have some significance. These factors were almost certain to have attracted the attention of the Celtic Druids who worshipped at the site.[2]

For almost 400 years the Celts of Britain remained immune to what was happening on the Continent, for there the Celtic peoples had been all but totally obliterated by the might of the Romans. More and more Celts must have poured across the English Channel to seek sanctuary with their British cousins as the Romans advanced up through Gaul, until the narrow stretch of water that separates the British Isles from the rest of Europe was all that maintained British independence. Gaius Julius Caesar (102 or 100–44 BC) first invaded Britain in 55 BC but was forced to retreat. He tried again and was likewise forced off the island. However, when he arrived for the third time, in 54 BC, he had the help of Androgeus, the nephew of the Celtic king Cassivellaunus, and thus defeated the Britons in a battle near present-day Canterbury. Cassivellaunus capitulated and agreed to pay tribute to Rome in return for remaining a vassal king. Julius Caesar agreed and departed. It was nearly a further century before Britain truly became a Roman province.

The Roman Invasion

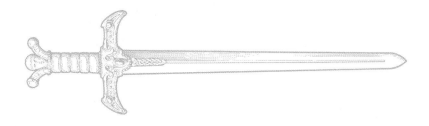

IN AD 43, at the instigation of the Roman Emperor Claudius (10 BC – AD 54), Britain finally fell to the Romans. Despite several uprisings against the Roman occupiers, notably that led by Boudicca, Queen of the Iceni, in AD 61,[1] the Celts soon fell to the might of the Romans and began to be systematically assimilated. Nowhere is this clearer than at the city of Bath, the Roman name for which was Aquae Sulis, or 'Waters of Sulis', Sulis being the name of a local Celtic deity.[2] Even though the Druids felt the brunt of Roman oppression and were all but obliterated, the normal Celtic people were simply governed with a strong hand, so that today a large number of Romano-Celtic artefacts remain. For over 350 years the Romans and the Celts lived together in England, though not always in peace.

The Romans, however, never crossed from Wales into Ireland, thus leaving the Goidelic Celts well alone, and never proceeded past the lowlands of Scotland, thanks to the ferocity of the Picts and Goidelic Celts who lived in the wilderness of the Scottish mountains. Instead, the Romans built a wall across the northernmost limit of their dominion, Hadrian's Wall (completed c.126), to keep these barbarian peoples at bay, though not always successfully, for the Picts overran and destroyed parts of the wall in 367, the wall itself not being repaired until 369 when the Picts were finally driven back from northern England and the Lowlands of Scotland.

In 410, after Alaric, King of the Goths, sacked Rome, dramatic changes were about to affect Britain as the Romans quickly departed in order to protect their homeland. For the first time in over 350 years the Celts felt able to reassert their old ways, which they undoubtedly did, and in the seven years between the departure of the Roman legions and the brief Roman second coming in 417 the Celts

Bronze Head of the
Emperor Claudius.
(British Museum.)

apparently totally reorganized, to the point where the Romans either could not
defeat them or could not be bothered to try, with their homeland under threat.
Britain was finally on its own and the people began to recover from their
oppression. Druidism appears to have been the first thing to spring back to life
and, under the leadership of the Druids, most of Britain seems to have once again
become Celtic. The euphoria was not to last long, for in 449 the first waves of a
new, more terrifying invader arrived on the southern shores of England.

The Anglo-Saxon Invasions

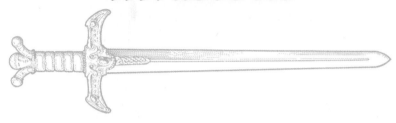

THE NEW INVADERS were the Angles, the Saxons and the Jutes. The first to come were the semi-legendary brothers Hengist and Horsa. They landed with their hordes at Ebbsfleet, on the Isle of Thanet, in 449, at the request of King Vortigern, who needed their help in a war against marauding Picts. In 455 the Saxons turned against Vortigern, but were defeated at Aylesford, where Horsa was killed. Hengist, however, continued the fight and was initially appeased when he was given Kent as his kingdom. But this did not satisfy the Saxons for long, and they soon set about eliminating all the Celts and pushing them further and further westwards. In 477 Aelle landed in Sussex and by 491 had conquered that region. Together the Angles and Saxons set about vanquishing vast tracts of Britain from the Celtic people.

Within 50 years or so of the first Anglo-Saxon landings, Britain's landscape had changed once more. Now, except for small pockets of resistance, most notably in Cornwall and Wales, Britain was an Anglo-Saxon country. In 494 the Jutes landed and added to the confusion, but still the Britons fought on. Having already suffered one long occupation, they did not relish the idea of once more being oppressed. It was this fighting that ultimately led to their downfall, for the Anglo-Saxon invaders were far better equipped for war and in almost every battle gained the upper hand and slaughtered many hundreds of Celts at a go. Yet the Britons fought on and on one occasion won a mighty victory over the invaders, at Mount Badon in c.490 or c.518,[1] though the exact site and date of the battle will never be known.

In 530 the Isle of Wight fell to Cerdic and from there the Saxons pressed on ever westwards, defeating the Britons at Deorham in 577. They were finally halted by the Britons at Faddiley in 583, a British victory that arrested their progress into

Bradbury Rings.
(Michael J. Stead.)

Wales. From that day to this, Wales has remained a bastion of Celtic tradition. Though the fighting did not really end until 829, when Egbert, King of Wessex, was recognized as the overlord of all England, true Celtdom in England had died out many years previously, some time during the sixth century, and was from then restricted to Cornwall and Wales.

The Birth of Arthur

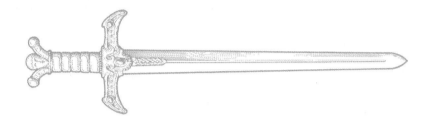

IT IS IN THE LIGHT of such overwhelming odds, and having sometimes gained the upper hand against the invading hordes, that the Celts first brought a single man to prominence, possibly the man who led the victorious Celts at the battle of Mount Badon.[1] Although the first references we have to this man date from many centuries later, he exhibits almost superhuman attributes. He was, of course, none other than King Arthur, though he would appear in the references to be a warlord or chieftain, his elevation to the ranks of monarchy not occurring until the local stories of his prowess and might were romanticized by medieval writers.

One has only to consider the plight of the Celts at that time to see the necessity for a 'super-hero' such as King Arthur. For almost 400 years their culture had been suppressed under the Romans. Then, almost at the eleventh hour, the Romans left and the Celts were able once again to establish their culture, only to have it even more ruthlessly oppressed by new bands of invaders.

Arthur appears to owe his name either to a corruption of the Roman *gens* name Artorius or, more likely, to the Celtic *artos viros* – 'bear man'. However, while today we know King Arthur as a single man, it seems likely that he is a composite figure made up of the best attributes of several of the Celtic heroes of the time. Now he is best known as the idealized chivalrous king described by Sir Thomas Malory (*d*. 1471) in his *Le Morte d'Arthur* (1470). Long before that, though, the persona of Arthur had begun its transition from local to national hero, and the inflation of his character had also begun to change from warrior to an almost godlike being. One notable example of this transition comes from a description of Arthur by Nennius (*fl*. 769) who says of the battle of Mount Badon that '960 of the enemy fell in a single attack by Arthur'. In fact, Nennius is one of the first literary sources actually to name Arthur, though he does not go so far as to call him a king, but rather *dux bellorum* – 'leader of battles'. The first coherent narrative of the life of King Arthur (now elevated to that lofty rank) appears in the fanciful eleventh century *Historia Regum Britanniae* by Geoffrey of Monmouth (*c.*1100–*c.*1154), a work that combines many of the earlier works along with Welsh folk-lore to give the Arthurian legends that are so widely known today.

It is perhaps interesting to note the Welsh influences on the retelling of the Arthurian legends, for this would seem to indicate that Arthur was a Welsh Celt who led his bands of warriors across the border to raid the Saxons before falling back to their strongholds in the Welsh mountains. In the same way as the Romans found the Scottish Highlands unassailable, so the Saxons appear to have found the mountains of South Wales impenetrable. Arthur – the historical Arthur that is – was obviously, therefore, a very good tactician as well as a born leader of men.

Arthur's fame as a leader and mighty warrior appears to have been widely known in northern Britain before any other region of the country. This statement hangs on a single line to be found in the *Gododdin*, a poem that is traditionally ascribed to the Welsh court poet Aneurin, who flourished in the late sixth and early seventh centuries. The poem celebrated the British heroes of Gododdin, a realm that stretched from the Forth to the Tees, who were annihilated by the Saxons in the bloody battle of Cattraith[2] *c.*600. In this poem the prowess of a Gododdin warrior is compared to Arthur:

> *He stabbed over three hundred of the finest,*
> *He glutted black ravens on the ramparts of the fort,*
> *Although he was no Arthur.*

The main problem with this poem is that the relevant line is now thought to be a possible later addition, but if it is original, this would indicate that Arthur had already been elevated from the ranks of warrior, at least in the north, by around 600 AD. It is certainly true that Arthur has numerous connections with Carlisle, which lies within what was the ancient kingdom of Rheged.[3]

No matter who Arthur was, or how he came into being, whether by history or by invention, his importance to the Celts was paramount, for, having been denied their homeland by force, they needed some hope, no matter how tenuous, that one day they would be able to reclaim the land that they rightly saw as rightfully theirs. Arthur was, and still is the very essence of the pseudo-mythical, semi-legendary super-hero who combines human and godly attributes. His elevation in rank from warrior to king serves only to magnify the reverence that the Celts felt for Arthur. He was their only hope, and even after that hope had been all but eroded, they gave themselves one final option, for the legends of Arthur clearly state that he will rise again. Therefore, Arthur became, to the early Celts, a Messiah who would deliver his oppressed people out of the hands of their Anglo-Saxon overlords and lead them, not only to victory, but also back into their very own promised land.

Thus was born King Arthur, though not the King Arthur we know today. That figure comes to us by an altogether different route. His is birth not through necessity but rather through poetry. The very first legends of Arthur must have been very simple indeed, for all they would have been were embroidered accounts of battles and feats of courage and daring. These feats have subsequently been grasped by storytellers, both ancient and modern, and altered beyond recognition to give us the mythologized view of Arthur as he is now.

The Origins of
the Round Table

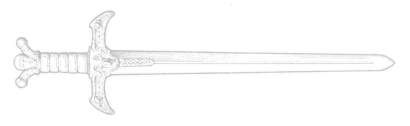

NOWHERE IS THIS TRANSITION more apparent than with the formation of an order of knights who were to become known as the Knights of the Round Table. But just how did this Round Table come into being?

The first literary reference to the Round Table is in the twelfth-century *Roman de Brut*, but this reference is particularly odd, for here the company of knights who were to gather at the table sat not around its perimeter but instead within the circle formed by the table, which would have, therefore, resembled a rather large doughnut. Why Wace (*c.*1115–*c.*1183), the Anglo-Norman poet who wrote of the table in this manner, should have placed the knights within the circle of the table remains a mystery. Thinking about it logically, why would anyone want to sit the knights within a circle so that they all faced outwards and thus away from each other.

Perhaps Wace was trying to allude to the very reasons for the establishment by Arthur of the order of the Round Table. Wace tells us that, during a feast at Camelot, the court of King Arthur, the barons quarrelled over precedence, which led to the death of several men. However, he does not elaborate any further and says simply that Arthur established the Round Table so that none should have precedence. This still does not explain the curious seating arrangement, which was possibly designed so that no one had to look into the face of another. This is pure supposition, but it remains a fascinating possibility.

Layamon (*fl.* thirteenth century), in his *Brut*, an amplified version of the *Roman de Brut* of Wace, goes further. He states that the quarrel broke out during a Christmas feast, and it was this that led to the establishment of the Round Table. According to Layamon, Arthur travelled to Cornwall a short time later and there met with a foreign carpenter who offered to make the king a table at which 1600 could sit with none having precedence over any of the others. Arthur immediately commissioned the table, which was completed and delivered within six weeks. This time the knights sat in the more normal position – that is around the outer edge.

Many, many other literary references to the Round Table exist. Robert de Boron (*fl.* 1200) says that the table could seat just 50, while the *Vulgate Version* states that the table could seat 250. Yet Layamon's figure of 1600 remains the largest by a long way. To combine with such a widely varying number of places at the table, there are just as many variations on its actual shape. Some authors make it a solid disc, others a doughnut, some make it a semicircle, others give it an opening so that servants might attend the knights from the centre of the table.

All this draws the student of Arthurian literature and the Arthurian legends deeper and deeper into a quandary, for just what is the truth behind the Round Table, and why was it to play such an important role in the legendary life of King Arthur and his company of knights? Perhaps we shall never know, but it seems that the table does have some historical foundation. Current thinking attributes the original ownership of the Round Table to King Leodegrance of Cameliard who passed it on to Arthur when he married Leodegrance's daughter Guinevere, along with 100 knights, and thus established the Knights of the Round Table. In this instance, it could seat 150, the final 50 knights of the company joining at various stages throughout the Arthurian legends.

However, another avenue of thought says that the Round Table was originally owned by Uther, under whose ownership it was known as the Old Table. Upon the death of Uther, the table passed into the custodianship of Leodegrance, who presented it to Arthur when that young man became king. The table is sometimes mentioned in the Italian romances as the Old Table, but it is not mentioned this way in any other European work. The Old Table was said to have been able to seat 50 in which case it was like the table mentioned by Robert de Boron. Perhaps de Boron was drawing on a tradition that none of the other writers was aware of, thus giving a much truer account of the table itself and of its origins.

One seldom mentioned aspect concerns the Table of the Wandering Companions. No complete description exists of this table, which was said to have accommodated those knights who were still in the process of proving their worth before being accepted as Knights of the Round Table. They would attend court on an irregular basis in between deeds of derring-do, after which they would return to recount their adventures to the Knights of the Round Table, who would then deliberate on the merit of these adventures and finally elect, possibly by a majority vote, those deemed worthy of elevation to the Round Table.

Some sources have sought to prove that the Round Table is a representation of both the solar year and the zodiac, though this belief would appear to stem from ancient bardic tradition.

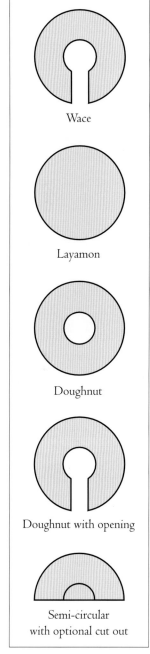

Wace

Layamon

Doughnut

Doughnut with opening

Semi-circular
with optional cut out

Designs of the Round Table
as found in various sources.

The Winchester Round Table. The thirteenth-century fake that hangs on the west wall of the Great Hall in Winchester Castle.

Apart from all the literary references to the Round Table, there remains one very tangible enigma – the Round Table that is hanging on the west wall of the Great Hall in Winchester Castle. For many years this table, some 5.5 metres (18 feet) in diameter, made of oak and weighing 1.25 tonnes, was thought to have been the actual Round Table from King Arthur's court. No one knows just how long it has actually been hanging there. It was first mentioned in John Hardyng's *Chronicle* of 1464 in which he describes the founding of the Order of the Round Table at Winchester, stating that the actual Round Table 'hangeth there yet'. However, the painting of King Arthur and the names of the principal knights that now adorn the table are of a later date than this, and it has now been established that the original painting was carried out in 1516, at the order of the young King Henry VIII, whose face appears as that of King Arthur. The present-day painting is the result of crude restoration work carried out on the table in 1789.

When the table was examined in more recent times it was discovered that it had indeed been built as a table, the legs later being cut away so that it could be wall-mounted. Later still it had been reinforced with planks, and then with a band of iron clamped all the way around it after the rim had been damaged by wet rot.

Close examination of the table also revealed a large number of holes that had been plugged with wine corks prior to the redecoration of 1789. These holes were mainly concentrated around the head of King Arthur and within the central rose decoration. The angle of the holes showed that it had been shot at while still hanging on the wall, the most likely culprits being Cromwellian soldiers who were barracked at Winchester in 1645.

When the table was X-rayed, it transpired, to everyone's surprise, that the painting of 1516 was the only one – the table had never been painted before that date. This proved a notable puzzle, for literary references abound to the decoration of the Round Table. The answer to this may have been revealed when the Victorian iron band around the rim of the table was removed, as underneath were discovered a large number of studs, exactly as one might expect would be needed to hold a painted cloth or leather skiver in place.

Modern dating techniques have proved beyond a shadow of doubt that this table dates from the thirteenth century and is therefore a fake. Dendro-chronological dating gave a felling date for the wood employed in the manufacture of the table as *c.*1250–5. This would appear to tally with the building in 1235 of the Great Hall at Winchester Castle, which for the next thirty years was decorated and furnished under the watchful eye of King Henry III, who may have once owned the original and had a copy made. Alternatively, it may be a slightly later addition, perhaps placed in the Great Hall by King Edward I, who had been present at Glastonbury during the reburial of the alleged remains of Arthur and Guinevere. The present-day table, even though it has now been conclusively proved to be a fake, does pose one very important question. If it is not the original, then is it an accurate copy?

The answer to this problem may lie in the fifteenth century (possibly earlier) Welsh work *Pedwar Marchog ar Hugan Llys Arthur*. This is remarkable in that it does not list the knights at King Arthur's court as the Knights of the Round Table, by which title they would surely have been known in the fifteenth century, but rather calls them the Twenty-four Knights of King Arthur's Court. It has been suggested that this work lists an order of knights that preceded the Knights of the Round Table, but this may not actually be the case, and it may be that the two orders are the same.

The reasoning behind this lies in the Winchester Round Table. This table is clearly divided into twenty-five segments – that is, one for each of the twenty-four knights, with the twenty-fifth reserved for King Arthur himself. Perhaps, therefore, the Round Table at Winchester can be looked at in a new light. It may well be a fake, but it is possibly a copy of the actual table, which has now sadly been lost to us.

All this is, of course, pure theory. But comparison of the list of knights given in the *Pedwar Marchog ar Hugan Llys Arthur* with those named on the Winchester Round

Table draws one closer and closer to the idea that the table is a true copy of the real thing. The Welsh text gives the twenty-four knights as:

> Gwalchmai* [the Welsh for Gawain], Drudwas, Eliwlod, Bors,* Perceval,* Galahad,* Lancelot,* Owain, Menw, Tristan,* Eiddilig, Nasiens, Mordred,* Hoel, Blaes, Cadog, Petroc, Morfran ab Tegid, Sanddef, Glewlwyd, Cyon, Aron, Llywarch Hàn and Bedwyr* [the Welsh for Bedivere].

Even though only those names marked with an asterisk (*) directly compare with the names on the Winchester Round Table, several important issues are raised. First, the names given in the Welsh text are just that, Welsh, though some have been Latinized in translation. During the fifteenth century, and indeed for many years previously, there had been a continuing conflict between the English and the Welsh. Therefore, it seems feasible that the copier of the Round Table simply changed the names to those that were more popularly known or accepted at that time. Also, if there had not actually been twenty-four knights seated around the table along with King Arthur, why did the copier, or faker as he would have been in this case, not make the number of places at the table suit the more popular renditions of the Arthurian legends that were current at the time.

There is, of course, no real answer, but it opens endless avenues of speculation, research and controversy until someone comes up with actual hard evidence to support one theory or another. What needs to be said is that there can be little doubt that there is some historical foundation to the Round Table and to its order of knights. Whether it was King Arthur – the historical Arthur – who instigated the building of the table, or adopted it from a predecessor or even from some Saxons he had conquered, is still another of the multitude of unfathomable and unanswerable questions that study of the Arthurian literature and legends throws up.

The Medieval Ideal of the Knights of the Round Table

THROUGH LITERATURE we can trace the development of King Arthur and his company, from their almost humble origins, in the midst of the Dark Ages, right up to the modern day. This clearly shows the transition from warrior to folk hero, and far beyond, so that today King Arthur can rightly rank alongside any other national hero, whether in Europe or across the rest of the world. It is this status that has led to the mass of literature that surrounds him and his company of knights.

Yet it is the medieval picture of King Arthur that sticks so vividly in most people's minds. Here we have knights in shining armour who ride magnificent steeds and do deeds of derring-do, rescuing maidens in distress, doing battle with dragons or other mythical beasts, and even travelling to the land of the dead and returning triumphant.

The truth is far different. The fifth- or sixth-century warriors would have been dressed far more simply. They had no gleaming suits of armour, and if they rode a horse, it was only because they were one of the fortunate, favoured few. Even kings at that time were known to walk into battle. So how does a warrior of such simple origins become so dramatically altered that he emerges as the leader of the most chivalrous order of knights ever known?

To answer this question it is necessary to look at when the majority of the Arthurian literature was written. This was the time of the Crusades, those fruitless expeditions sanctioned by the Pope to recover Palestine from the Muslims. The first Crusade started in 1095, and for almost 200 years Christian armies were led into battle in the Middle East. Those who went on the Crusades were thought of as heroes by the Church, though not necessarily by the general population. Here we have knights in shining armour, riding to foreign, far-off lands to do battle with

Above: Bronze helmet crest in the shape of a boar. (British Library.)

Left: One of many seals used by the Knights Templar. (British Library.)

non-Christians and heretics. Such is the very essence of legend, and it was against this background that the core of Arthurian literature was written.

Poets of the time obviously likened King Arthur to the crusading kings, and equally equated their company of knights with the Knights of the Round Table. If those knights going off to fight for Christianity were true knights, then those who had, in times gone past, sought to protect Britain against heathen invaders must also be honourable and chivalrous. Two contemporary orders of knights from the relevant period may easily be likened to the Knights of the Round Table. These were the Knights Templar, or Knights of the Temple of Solomon, who were founded in 1119 in Jerusalem and took solemn religious vows; and the Knights of St John, or Knights Hospitallers of St John of Jerusalem, the oldest order of Christian chivalry (founded in Jerusalem *c.*1048), who took their name from the hospital of St John in Jerusalem.

The Knights Templar were suppressed and disbanded *c.*1308–12, but the Knights of St John survive to this day and have their headquarters in the Palazzo di Malta, Rome, established in 1798 after they were expelled from Malta by Napoleon. The Grand Master of this order of knights is today the world's highest-ranking Roman Catholic lay person.

So what exactly makes a chivalrous knight, and how do the real-life chivalrous knights correspond to the Knights of the Round Table? Chivalry itself was based on four basic tenets, which may be summed up simply as covering all aspects of righteousness: blamelessness, equity, ethicalness, faithfulness, goodness, honesty, honour, integrity, justice, morality, probity, purity, rectitude, uprightness and virtue. Any or all of these words can quite easily sum up a part of chivalry, which can additionally encompass courage, courtesy, courtliness, gallantry, gentlemanliness, knighthood and politeness. It is not surprising, therefore, that some of the Knights of the Round Table failed to live up to such high expectations.

The first tenet of chivalry, courage, regarded war as a positive, enriching experience. The knight was therefore a fighting man first and foremost, and it was the duty of the knight to be seen to fight fairly. Any atrocities could be left to the common fighting man, for if a knight were to stoop to fighting outside the realms of the unwritten code of chivalry, then that knight would be shunned, or banished, or possibly even demoted to a commoner's rank. Even knights of enemy countries were held in such great esteem that they were allowed to attend jousts and tournaments, and were given safe passage both to and from the contests.

The second tenet of chivalry was honour. In one classic example, though the woman in question was hideous beyond belief, Sir Gawain promised to marry her after she had helped King Arthur. Sir Gawain saw his promise through, though when he did he was justly rewarded as the ugly old crone turned into the most beautiful of maidens. This story is, of course, the fantasy of the authors of the legends, but serves to illustrate the lengths to which a knight was expected to go in the pursuit of honour, for it was not only his honour but the honour of his comrades that was at stake if he reneged on any promise.

The third tenet was justice, an aspect that featured almost as widely as honour in the Arthurian legends. The whole principle of the Round Table itself was based on justice, for King Arthur thought it unjust that any single knight within his company should be considered, or consider himself, better than any other member.

The fourth and final tenet of chivalry, the one most widely used within the context of the Arthurian legends, concerned the conduct of a knight in respect of those in need of assistance. History records many instances of two fighting knights breaking off and aiding a commoner before coming back to the field of battle to fight to the death. Likewise, if, during the course of combat, one knight were to get into difficulties – say, his horse became bogged down in mud – then the other knight would break off to give him assistance in all friendship. Yet once both were back on equal terms, the fight would recommence and usually end with the death of one, or indeed, on many occasions, both of the knights.

Tournaments of this nature feature in the Arthurian legends, but taking things even further, for the main chivalry of the Arthurian knights concerned the fairer sex. A knight was often immediately dispatched if a maiden was in distress, even though it might have been a ruse to lure the knight into a trap. This did not matter, for the code of chivalry that the medieval writers imposed on the Knights of the Round Table, meant that they would gladly ride off to assist a maiden in distress, real or imaginary. This aspect was used on occasion to trap knights, who usually came into contact with dishonoured knights whom they always managed to defeat, thus upholding all the tenets of chivalry in a single act.

The Quest for the Holy Grail

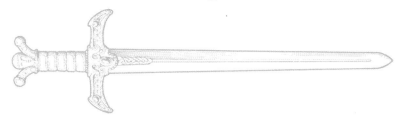

THERE IS, PERHAPS, no better example of the chivalrous lengths to which the Arthurian knights were made to go thanks to the imaginations of the medieval writers than the quest for the Holy Grail, for in this only the purest of knights could accomplish their end. All past sins were taken into account, a singular fact that ruled out the unfortunate Sir Lancelot, though the medieval writers obviously had a soft spot for him – even though he was never to achieve the Grail, they did at least allow him a sight of it. All the knights who took part in the quest underwent marvellous adventures, adventures that were indeed worthy of the Knights of the Round Table, and yet many of them have nothing whatsoever to do with the goal the knights were seeking. They are simply there to embroider the story, and to prove the might of chivalry, for good will always overcome evil.

The basis of the quest story appears to come from a much earlier Celtic tradition. The word 'grail' is derived from the Old French *graal*, meaning a type of dish. It is first mentioned in the works of Chrétien de Troyes, although he does not refer to the Holy Grail but to the object of the quest as 'the grail', a common noun. It was not until later that the object of the quest became '*the* Grail'.

Although in its final incarnation the Grail has become the chalice cup of the Last Supper, its origins are not so simple to determine. Connection has been sought between the Grail of Arthurian legend and the chalice supposedly brought to Britain by Jesus's uncle, Joseph of Arimathea. However, the magical qualities of the Grail stories suggest a much older, Otherworldly connection. King Arthur's expedition to the Otherworld to obtain a magical cauldron as recorded in the *Preiddeu Annwfn*[1] seems to reflect the ability of the Grail to provide inexhaustible sustenance. This story has a direct parallel in the story of *Culhwch and Olwen*,[2] and both have aspects that directly relate to the Grail quest as it is known today.

The Bertinus Chalice (1222)
now in the Metropolitan
Museum of Art in NYC. One
of several cups believed to be
the Holy Grail. (Steven Brown.)

Therefore, either or both, may have been the originals, and thus the magical
cauldron of Celtic tradition becomes transformed into the symbolic cup of the
Holy Eucharist. It seems wholly appropriate, therefore, that the medieval writers
who told the story of the quest for the Holy Grail should apply to it the most
chivalrous order of knights that mankind was ever likely to know, for the
underlying theme of seeking mystical union with God was appropriate for the times
when the Crusades were in full swing.

Thus the medieval writers took hold of the Arthurian knights and elevated them
from merciless warriors, for that is what they surely would have been in the fifth
and sixth centuries, and 600 years or more later turned them into the ideal of a
chivalrous order of knights whose sole purpose was to right wrong and to fight for
king, for country and for Christendom. But then, that is what the true fifth- and
sixth-century knights would have been doing anyway, although possibly not in such
a refined manner as the medieval writers would have them do it. Regrettably, for the
true student of ancient history or the origins of the legends, this does little to give
an accurate insight into what the knights must truly have been like. It does,
however, enable us to realize just what it must have been like for a knight of the
eleventh or twelfth century, and allows us to understand, just slightly better, why
the Crusades were fought, for Christianity was under threat, and no honour-bound,
chivalrous knight could, by his own code of ethics, stand by and do nothing.

The Knights of the
Round Table

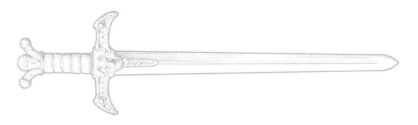

ALTHOUGH PART TWO – the main section of this book – covers the careers of many of the Knights of the Round Table at some length, those profiled are by no means all of the Knights of the Round Table, so we must spend a little time here looking at those others who made it to that illustrious company but are not profiled. For the sake of completeness, members of the orders of knights referred to as the Twenty-four Knights of King Arthur's Court and as Knights of the Old Table have been included.

One thing that does become very apparent from the study of this list is just how many knights became Knights of the Round Table through relationship. There is no better illustration of this nepotistic trait than the genealogy of the House of Lot (see opposite), for Lot is the progenitor of more Knights of the Round Table than any other character within the Arthurian legends, except for Sir Pellinore, though in the latter case not all of that knight's knightly progeny are always named as his offspring. However, in the simple genealogy illustrated (see opposite), Sir Pellinore fathered eight knights, while his daughter married a ninth. This in itself raises a worthy point. Even though Arthur might have been the king who sat at the head of the Round Table, the genealogy of the House of Lot would seem to suggest that the driving force behind that illustrious order of knights was one of Arthur's vassal kings.

THE HOUSE OF LOT

Lot was married to Arthur's half-sister Morgause, by way of Igraine's first marriage to Gorlois, Duke of Cornwall. Lot fathered on Morgause no fewer than six of the

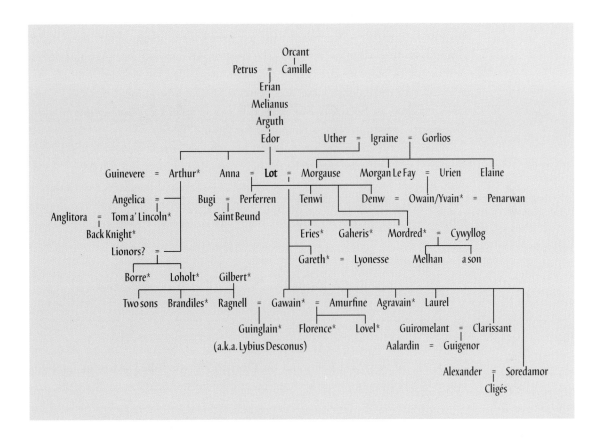

The House of Lot

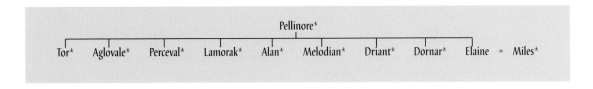

Sir Pellinore

* = Knight of the Round Table

most prominent of the Knights of the Round Table, including the treacherous Sir Mordred, though the legends usually account for the birth of this dark figure through an unwitting incestuous relationship Arthur had with his half-sister. Arthur, on the other hand, as illustrated in this genealogy, fathered just four knights who came to the Round Table, and none of these is a prominent member. Many other children are accredited to Arthur, but none of these, possibly due to their illegitimacy, was to become a Knight of the Round Table.

When second and subsequent generations who also made it to the Round Table are included, Lot can be seen to be the major supplier of loyal and chivalrous blood. Perhaps even the Round Table once belonged to Lot and may have been used by that king in much the same way as Arthur employed it. This, however, is pure supposition and there is no evidence, literary or otherwise, to support it.

Sir Adragain

A pious knight who, after the death of King Arthur, became a hermit.

Sir Aglovale

A son of Sir Pellinore and brother of Sir Perceval, Sir Lamorak, Sir Alan, Sir Melodian, Sir Tor, Sir Driant and Sir Dornar. He was killed when Sir Lancelot rescued Queen Guinevere, who was about to be burned at the stake for treason.

Sir Agravain

The brother of Gawain. Agravain, Mordred and 12 other knights sought to trap Lancelot with Guinevere. He and the other 12 knights were killed by the unarmed Lancelot, leaving only Mordred alive to report Guinevere's infidelity to Arthur. Other stories say that Agravain survived, only to be killed when Sir Lancelot rescued Guinevere after she had been condemned to death for adultery.

Sir Alan

One of the eight Knights of the Round Table who were sons of Sir Pellinore, his brothers being Sir Aglovale, Sir Perceval, Sir Lamorak, Sir Melodian, Sir Tor, Sir Driant and Sir Dornar.

Sir Alon

A grandnephew of King Arthur who appears to have relied on nepotism to secure his seat at the Round Table.

Sir Aron

Simply named in the *Pedwar Marchog ar Hugan Llys Arthur* as one of the Twenty-four Knights of King Arthur's Court. Nothing more is known about him.

Sir Artegall

Also known as Artgualchar by Geoffrey of Monmouth, Artegall is described as the First Earl or Count of Guarensis (Warwick), though Spenser (*c.*1552–99) makes him the son of King Cador of Cornwall who bore the arms of the classical Achilles into battle. This would seem to suggest that he was almost invincible in battle, as indeed was Achilles, but that he had one weak spot, his very own Achilles' heel.

Sir Bagdemagus

The King of Gore[1] and a cousin of Arthur. Described as a benign knight who took offence at nothing, he did take umbrage when Sir Tor was welcomed to the Round Table ahead of him. However, this did not prevent him from stopping his son Meleagaunce raping Guinevere after Meleagaunce had carried off the queen. Sir Bagdemagus took part in the quest for the Holy Grail, but mistakenly carried a shield with a red cross on it that was intended for Sir Galahad. For this he was wounded by a mysterious White Knight and eventually killed by Sir Gawain.

Sir Balin and Sir Balan

Two brothers who originated from Northumberland, Sir Balan being the younger of the two. Sir Balin at first incurred King Arthur's displeasure by killing the Lady of the Lake who had come to Arthur's court to request the boon he had promised her when she gave him Excalibur, that boon being the head of Sir Balin.[2] Sir Balin arrived and recognized the Lady of the Lake as the fairy who had killed his mother, so he cut off her head. Arthur banished him, but he succeeded in capturing one of Arthur's enemies and was thus made a Knight of the Round Table along with his brother. Unwittingly, the two brothers were forced into combat, neither recognizing the other – not, that is, until each had received a mortal wound.

Sir Banin

Little is known about this knight other than that he was a godson of King Ban of Brittany.[3]

Sir Baudwin

One of the very first knights of King Arthur's company, he was, at the start of King Arthur's reign, made a constable of the realm. Later he was made one of the governors of Britain during Arthur's war with the Roman Empire, but ended his life as a physician and hermit, presumably as penance for failing to stop the usurping schemes of Sir Mordred.

Sir Belleus

A Knight of the Round Table who came to that illustrious order after he had been knighted by Sir Lancelot to atone for an unfortunate incident in which Sir Lancelot came across Belleus's pavilion and went to bed there. Belleus arrived some time later and climbed into bed alongside Sir Lancelot, whom he mistook for his sleeping lover and embraced. Sir Lancelot awoke and wounded Belleus, but when the truth came out, Sir Lancelot made Belleus a Knight of the Round Table.

Sir Belliance

Yet another of the Knights of the Round Table who had an unbridled hatred for Sir Lancelot. In the company of Sir Griflet, Sir Belliance set off in pursuit of Sir Lancelot at the bequest of King Arthur after Sir Lancelot had made good his escape from Camelot, having been discovered in the bedchamber of the queen.

Sir Blaes

The son of the Earl of Llychlyn[4] and one of the Twenty-four Knights of King Arthur's Court.

Sir Blamore de Ganis

The son of Sir Lancelot and brother of Sir Bleoberis. On one occasion he accused King Anguish[5] of murder, only to be subsequently defeated in combat by Tristan, King Anguish's champion. Afterwards Sir Blamore de Ganis and Sir Tristan became firm friends. During the quarrel between Sir Lancelot and King Arthur, Sir Blamore de Ganis and his brother naturally supported their father and as a result Sir Blamore de Ganis was made the Duke of Limousin. Following the death of King Arthur, Sir Blamore de Ganis followed the same route as a number of his comrades and became a hermit.

Sir Bleoberis

One of the sons of Sir Lancelot and the brother of Sir Blamore de Ganis. Sir Bleoberis supported his father in his quarrel with King Arthur and was rewarded by being made the Duke of Poitiers. Sir Bleoberis went on to join in the Holy Crusades, but what became of him remains unknown.

Sir Borre

One of the illegitimate sons of Arthur who was made a Knight of the Round Table when he came of age, his investiture again possibly relying on nepotism.

Sir Brandiles

The son of Sir Gilbert, though sometimes named as the son of Lac, who entered into combat with Sir Gawain after that knight had defeated his father and his two brothers, as well as seducing his sister. After a while the fight was stopped to be resumed at a later date, but in an early work[6] the two knights' paths never crossed again. A later text,[7] however, does make their paths cross, but during the continuation of their fight the ghostly image of Sir Brandiles's sister appears, along with her son by Gawain, Guinglain, and the fight is once more stopped, this time for good.

Sir Brastias

Having originally served the Duke of Cornwall, Sir Brastias swore his allegiance to the new king, fought against the rebellion that rose up against King Arthur at the start of his reign and was rewarded by being made the warden of the north of England.

Sir Breunis Saunce Pyté

A magical knight who appears to have had the ability to be in more than one place at once. His loyalty to Arthur was not complete and he turned against his former ally, but was killed in combat by Sir Gareth.

Sir Breunor

Better known as Sir Breunor the Black, the brother of Sir Daniel and Sir Dinadan, his story may be found under the profile of the Black Knight (see pages 77–9).

Sir Brian des Iles

Perhaps identical with Brandiles in origin, Brian des Iles attacked Arthur's kingdom with the help of Sir Kay, but was defeated and subsequently swore an oath of allegiance and was made Arthur's steward, presumably after Sir Kay had been removed from that position – a position he had held since Arthur came to the throne – as punishment for aiding Sir Brian des Iles, or perhaps because Sir Kay was killed during the conflict.

Sir Brunor

A Knight of the Old Table about whom very little is known, as he is simply described as one of the best knights of that order and is, therefore, perhaps a shining example of the chivalrous ideal. It is quite possible that he is none other than the Sir Breunor who appears as one of the Knights of the Round Table.

Sir Cadog

Simply named as one of the Twenty-four Knights of King Arthur's Court.

Sir Carados

The son of a sorceress and the brother of Sir Turquine. Carados took Sir Gawain captive and threw him into a dungeon, but he was killed by Sir Lancelot, who then released Sir Gawain and Carados's other captives.

Sir Carl of Carlisle

Turned into a giant by some enchantment, Sir Carl once welcomed and entertained Sir Gawain and Sir Kay. At Sir Carl's request, Sir Kay beheaded him and so broke the spell, restoring Sir Carl to his normal size. Sir Gawain subsequently married his daughter and Arthur welcomed him to the court and knighted him, making him the Lord of Carlisle, hence his epithet. However, some say that he took the name Carl only after he had become the Lord of Carlisle, while other dubious references say that Carlisle was named in his honour.

Sir Claris

The hero of the thirteenth-century French verse romance *Claris et Laris*, in which he rescued his companion Laris from Tallas, the King of Denmark, after which he married Laris's sister, Lidoine, and was rewarded for his courage by being made a Knight of the Round Table.

Sir Cligés

The hero of *Cligés*, a romance written *c.*1164 by Chrétien de Troyes, Cligés was the son of Alexander, Emperor of Constantinople, and Soredamor, the daughter of Lot. He came to Arthur's court in self-imposed exile and was knighted, but later returned to his native Constantinople after the death of his uncle.

Sir Colgrevance

A native of Gore who was possibly made a Knight of the Round Table at the same time as his king, Sir Bagdemagus. Accounts of Sir Colgrevance's death vary. In one he was killed by Sir Lionel, yet in another he was among those knights who surprised Sir Lancelot and Guinevere together and was killed by the escaping unarmed Lancelot.

Sir Cyon

One of the Twenty-four Knights of King Arthur's Court.

Sir Dagonet

Originally King Arthur's fool, he was elevated to the Knights of the Round Table by King Arthur as a reward for his services, though what the other knights thought about having the court jester number among them is, regrettably, not recorded, although it does conjure up a very amusing picture.

Sir Damas

The brother of Sir Ontzlake, who used to trap other knights and then force them to do combat with him, a practice that King Arthur quickly stopped.

Sir Daniel

The brother of Sir Dinadan and one of those knights who trapped Sir Lancelot and Guinevere together in the queen's bedchamber, but was killed by the escaping Lancelot. As Sir Breunor is also named as a brother of Sir Dinadan, it seems quite likely that Sir Daniel was also a brother of Sir Breunor, though it has been suggested that Sir Daniel and Sir Breunor were simply different names for the same character.

Sir Dinadan

The brother of Sir Daniel and Sir Breunor the Black. He is reputed to have seen no sense in fighting for fighting's sake, but was quick to take up arms against the rebelling Sir Mordred, by whom he was killed.

Sir Dinas

The seneschal (steward) of King Mark,[8] who pitied the plight of Sir Tristan and became that sorry knight's companion. Later he accompanied Sir Lancelot when he rescued Guinevere and was duly made the Duke of Anjou. After the death of King Mark, at least according to the fourteenth-century Italian verse romance *Tavola ritonda*, Sir Dinas was made the King of Cornwall.

Sir Dirac

The brother of Sir Lac.

Sir Dodinel

Known as 'The Savage' after his penchant for hunting wild game in the forests, some authorities have sought to make him the original of Sir Perceval.

Sir Dornar

A son of Sir Pellinore and brother of Sir Driant, Sir Perceval, Sir Aglovale, Sir Alan, Sir Tor, Sir Lamorak and Sir Melodian. His sister, Elaine, married Sir Miles.

Sir Driant

One of the eight knightly sons of Sir Pellinore. Sir Driant died after a mortal wound had been inflicted on him in combat with Sir Gawain.

Sir Drudwas

The son of King Tryffin of Denmark and one of the Twenty-four Knights of King Arthur's Court. On one occasion he was to meet King Arthur in combat but, being a devious knight, he sent his three pet griffins along ahead of him and instructed them to kill the first man that came on to the field of combat. However, King Arthur was delayed by Drudwas's sister, the king's mistress, so Sir Drudwas was the first to arrive and was killed by his own pets when they failed to recognize him.

Sir Ector

A Knight of the Old Table, the father of Sir Kay and the foster father of King Arthur, who was placed in his care by Merlin shortly after his birth. Sir Ector accompanied both Arthur and Kay to the tournament in London where Arthur recovered the Sword in the Stone, and made Sir Kay tell the truth after he had at first claimed that it was he who had removed the sword. Nothing more is heard of Sir Ector after the coronation of King Arthur.

Sir Ector de Maris

The brother of Sir Lancelot, he was taken captive by Sir Turquine, who wanted to kill Sir Lancelot, and duly rescued by his brother. He later succeeded his father as the King of Brittany.

Sir Eiddilig

One of the Twenty-four Knights of King Arthur's Court.

Sir Eliwlod

One of the Twenty-four Knights of King Arthur's Court, the grandson of Uther and nephew of King Arthur. Seen by some as the original for Sir Lancelot, Eliwlod appeared to King Arthur in the guise of an eagle after his death.[9]

Sir Erec

The son of Sir Lac, Erec is the hero of *Erec et Enide* by Chrétien de Troyes. In this, Erec gave up his knightly adventures after he married Enide, but she scolded him for doing so and he undertook more.

Sir Eries

A son of Lot[10] and perhaps the original of the little mentioned Sir Gaheris, though the two are usually named as brothers in the traditional genealogies.

Sir Evadeam

A man who fell under an enchantment and became a dwarf. Sir Gawain, meanwhile, had been told that he would assume the form of the next man he met. He came across Evadeam and, while Evadeam resumed his normal form, Sir Gawain became a dwarf. Evadeam then set about releasing Sir Gawain from the enchantment and was made a Knight of the Round Table as a reward for restoring Sir Gawain to his former self.

Sir Fergus

There are two knights by this name in the Arthurian legends. One was a ploughboy who aspired to become a knight, which he finally did when, after many adventures on his horse, Arondiel, he married the Lady of Lothian. The other Fergus was a Knight of the Round Table of Cornish provenance who was said to have killed a Black Knight who guarded a wimple and a horn on an ivory lion.

Sir Ferragunze

A knight who swore to Arthur that he was never jealous of his wife, Verseria. To test him, Arthur arranged for Verseria to be discovered in the arms of Sir Gawain. True to his word, Ferragunze showed no signs of jealousy and simply excused himself.

Sir Florence

The son of Sir Gawain. He was one of the knights who trapped Guinevere and Lancelot together, but was killed while the latter made good his escape.

Sir Galahad

Not the same Sir Galahad as profiled later (see pages 87–91) but rather one of the Twenty-four Knights of King Arthur's Court. It has been argued that the two are identical, but it is now reasoned that this Galahad is actually the origin of Sir Lancelot, father of the more famous Sir Galahad.

Sir Galehaut

The son of Sir Brunor and the giantess Bagota, Galehaut was the ruler of the District Isles, which remain unidentified, Surluse,[11] and several other kingdoms. He invaded Britain but was befriended by Sir Lancelot. Through that friendship he also became a friend of King Arthur, who made him a Knight of the Round Table. When he thought that Sir Lancelot was dead, he fasted until the illness that resulted killed him.

Sir Galeron

A Scottish knight whose Galloway lands were confiscated by King Arthur (why is not disclosed), but he then swore allegiance to Arthur and was created a Knight of the Round Table.

Sir Gales li Caus

According to Gerbert,[12] this knight was the husband of Philosophine and the father by her of Sir Perceval.

Sir Galihodin

A cousin of Sir Galehaut and the ruler of Surluse, one of his cousin's kingdoms. He was made the Duke of Sentoge by Sir Lancelot after he had joined that knight in his flight from King Arthur's court.

Sir Gilbert

The father of Brandiles (though Brandiles is sometimes named as the son of Lac), two other sons and a daughter, who was, depending on which source is consulted, named either Jeschuté or Ragnell. The latter name was used when this daughter had an affair with Sir Gawain and bore him a son, Sir Guinglain.

Sir Glewlwyd

Named as one of the Twenty-four Knights of King Arthur's Court, Glewlwyd is more normally found as the gatekeeper or porter of King Arthur's court, to whom the epithet *gafaelfawr* ('great grasp') is usually applied.

Sir Gornemant de Goort

Prince of the unidentified kingdom of Graherz and father of three sons, Gurzgi, Lascoyt and Schentefleurs, all of whom met violent deaths, as well as a single daughter, Liaze. He hoped Sir Perceval, whom he trained, would marry Liaze, but this did not come about.

Sir Griflet

Having his origins in the Celtic deity Gilfaethwy,[13] Griflet was, in some versions of the story of Arthur's last battle, charged with returning Excalibur to the Lady of the Lake, a task that is normally ascribed to Sir Bedivere. Having seen King Arthur's tomb, Sir Griflet became a hermit but died shortly afterwards. Another story tells how he and Sir Belliance set off after Sir Lancelot at the request of King Arthur, to bring Sir Lancelot back to Camelot to answer the charge of treason after he had been discovered in the bedchamber of Queen Guinevere.

Sir Guinglain

The illegitimate son of Gawain whose true identity was kept from him by his mother, Ragnell, the loathsome hag Gawain had been honour bound to marry after she had helped King Arthur answer the riddle 'What is it that a lady desires most?' Thus, when he came to Arthur's court, he was nicknamed Lybius Desconus, or Le Bel Inconnu, both roughly meaning 'The Fair Unknown One'. He was dispatched by Arthur to the aid of a princess who had been changed into a snake by sorcery. Having defeated a treacherous knight, Guinglain laid down to sleep and in that sleep was embraced by a snake, which told him of his parentage. When he awoke he found that the snake had become a beautiful princess and his quest had been accomplished. He subsequently married the princess.

Sir Hoel

One of the Twenty-four Knights of King Arthur's Court who is sometimes named as the first husband of Igraine,[14] though this role is normally taken by Gorlois.

Sir Ironside

A scurrilous knight, more commonly known as the Red Knight of the Red Lands, who laid siege to the maiden Lyonesse, but was defeated by Sir Gareth, who then married Lyonesse.

Sir Kamelin

An Irish knight, the son of the Irish King Alvrez and the brother of Miroet.

Sir Lac

The brother of Dirac, King of Estregales and ruler of the unidentified Black Isles, Lac was the father of Erec, Brandiles and the maiden Jeschuté, though Brandiles is sometimes named as the son of Sir Gilbert.

Sir Lamorak

The son of Sir Pellinore and brother of Sirs Perceval, Aglovale, Alan, Melodian, Tor, Driant and Dornar. Lamorak was killed by Sir Gawain after he had slept with Morgause, Gawain's mother.

Sir Lionel

The brother of Sir Bors, Lionel was given the throne of Gaul by Arthur but was, following the death of Arthur, killed by Mordred's son Melehan.

Sir Llywarch Hên

A celebrated Welsh poet who is thought to have flourished c.600 and whose epithet Hên means 'the old'. Sometimes associated with Taliesin,[15] Llywarch Hên is listed as one of the Twenty-four Knights of King Arthur's Court, but it is now thought that he is a relatively late addition to that list.

Sir Lohengrin

A Teutonic knight who was said to have been the son of Sir Perceval in the Germanic romances, though he sometimes features as the son of Sir Lancelot. In these he sailed to the aid of a princess in the guise of a swan in a boat drawn by an angel. He duly rescued the maiden and married her but made her promise never to ask his name. She kept her promise for a number of years, but eventually could resist no longer. Immediately Lohengrin disappeared and remarried, but was killed by mercenaries sent by his new wife's parents, who believed that their daughter was under his spell.

Sir Loholt

One of the sons of Arthur whose mother remains in doubt. As little is ever said about Loholt, it would appear that he owes his place at the Round Table to his father. One story says that he was murdered by Sir Kay.

Sir Lovel

One of the sons of Sir Gawain, and one of those who was killed by the unarmed Lancelot after he had been caught *in flagrante delicto* with Guinevere.

Sir Lucan

The Duke of Gloucester, the brother of Bedivere and Arthur's butler. Following the battle of Camlann, at which Arthur received his mortal wound, Lucan and Bedivere attempted to lift the dying king. Being badly wounded himself, the effort killed Lucan. A variant says that the dying king embraced Lucan and it was the strength of this embrace that killed him.

Sir Luguain

The servant of Yder whose loyalty was repaid when he was created a Knight of the Round Table.

Sir Lybius Desconus

'The Fair Unknown One', the illegitimate son of Gawain whose true identity was hidden from him by his mother. Lybius Desconus is actually a nickname, and this character is in fact the same as Sir Guinglain (see page 49).

Sir Mador

One of the participants in the quest for the Holy Grail. He appears at one time to have served as the gatekeeper of Camelot, as he is usually given the epithet *de la Porte* – 'of the door'. He also features in the story of Guinevere's affair with Sir Lancelot, accusing the queen of treason. She is proved innocent when she is championed by Sir Bors, and Sir Mador is beaten in single combat by Sir Lancelot (see pages 113–20).

Sir Marrok

For some unknown reason this knight was changed into a werewolf for seven years by his wife.

Sir Meleagaunce

The scurrilous son of Sir Bagdemagus who, on one occasion, abducted Queen Guinevere and was stopped from raping her only by the intervention of his father. Sir Lancelot and Meleagaunce fought in single combat, but the fight was stopped when Sir Bagdemagus beseeched Guinevere to have the life of his son spared. The two combatants were to meet a year later, but again the fight was stopped. There are several different endings to the story of Sir Meleagaunce, but all of them seem to agree that he was finally killed by Sir Lancelot.

Sir Melodian

One of the eight knightly sons of Sir Pellinore whose brothers were Sirs Aglovale, Perceval, Lamorak, Alan, Tor, Driant and Dornar.

Sir Menw

Named as one of the Twenty-four Knights of King Arthur's Court, Sir Menw, whose name is more fully Menw fab Teirgwaedd (his epithet means 'son of Teirgwaedd'), appears in early Welsh texts as a sorcerer.

Sir Miles

The knightly lover, some say husband, of Elaine, the daughter of Sir Pellinore. After Sir Miles was killed, Elaine committed suicide.

Sir Miroet

A son of the Irish King Alvrez and brother of Kamelin.

Sir Nascien

During the Grail Quest this knight was blinded for coming too close to the Grail, but was cured by drops of blood that came from the Lance of Longinus.[16] It appears that Nascien was the Christian name he adopted after he had been converted, for he is recorded originally as having been named Seraphe.

Sir Nasiens

One of the Twenty-four Knights of King Arthur's Court. It now seems likely that he was the origin of Sir Nascien.

Sir Ontzlake

The younger brother of the evil Sir Damas.

Sir Owain the Bastard

The half-brother of Owain (see page 156), whom his father, Urien,[17] fathered on the wife of his seneschal (steward). Noted for his common sense, Owain the Bastard was killed in a joust by Sir Gawain, who failed to recognize him.

Sir Palamedes

A pagan knight who fought Sir Tristan for the hand of Iseult. He converted to Christianity the instant Sir Tristan knocked his sword from his hand. The fight was stopped, never to be resumed, and Palamedes eventually became the Duke of Provence.

Sir Pedivere

Having killed his own wife, Sir Pedivere was made to carry the body of his wife by Sir Lancelot and seek the forgiveness of Guinevere. He eventually became a hermit.

Sir Pelleas

An unfortunate knight who became enamoured with Ettard, but she did not reciprocate his feelings. Sir Gawain said he would help, but instead bedded Ettard himself. However, Nimue, the Lady of the Lake, cast two spells, the first of which made Ettard fall in love with Pelleas, but the second of which made Pelleas fall in love with Nimue. Finding herself in the very position that Pelleas had originally found himself in, Ettard died of a broken heart.

Sir Pellinore

A subordinate king to Arthur who is variously described as the ruler of the unidentified kingdoms of Listinoise and the Gaste Forest, or Northumberland. Some sources say that he was eventually killed by Sir Gawain. His family tree (see page 39) shows him to have been a very important supplier of knights to the Round Table, for he fathered eight sons, all of whom became Knights of the Round Table, and one daughter, who married another of the order. His daughter is named as Elaine and her husband as Sir Miles. His sons were Sirs Aglovale, Perceval, Lamorak, Alan, Melodian, Tor, Driant and Dornar.

Sir Petroc

One of the Twenty-four Knights of King Arthur's Court. He appears to have his origins in the Cornish Saint Petroc and was reputed to have been one of the seven survivors of the battle of Camlann, Arthur's last battle, though sources differ on the actual number of survivors. Another account of Sir Petroc's death may be found in the profile of Sir Bors (see pages 81–51).

Sir Phelot

A treacherous knight who contrived a plan to kill Sir Lancelot. He persuaded his wife to beseech Sir Lancelot to rescue her hawk from a tree. Lancelot immediately sprang into action, even though to climb the tree he had to remove his armour. Seeing his opportunity, Sir Phelot rode out of his hiding place and attacked the unarmed Lancelot, but that knight took hold of a stout branch, repelled the attack, knocked Sir Phelot from his horse and then killed him with his own sword.

Sir Polidamas

The nephew of Sir Yder.

Sir Priamus

Originally a Saracen[18] knight whose line of descent was said to include the biblical Joshua, Alexander the Great, the Maccabees and Hector of Troy! He fought Sir Gawain and then asked that knight to help him to convert to Christianity, following which he was made a duke and welcomed to the Knights of the Round Table.

Sir Raynbrown

The son of Sir Ironside.

Sir Sagremor

A descendant of the imperial family of Constantinople and the son of the King of Hungary.

Sir Sandav

The most beautiful of Arthur's knights. He took part in, and survived, the battle of Camlann. His survival was the result of his beauty, as people mistook him for an angel and no one dared attack him. Sir Sandav is yet another example of opposing aspects in Celtic myth and legend, his beauty being offset at the battle of Camlann by the ugliness of Sir Morfran ab Tegid (see pages 139–41).

Sir Sanddef

One of the Twenty-four Knights of King Arthur's Court. He is in all probability the original Sir Sandav.

Sir Segurant the Brown

A knight of the Old Table, Uther's mightiest warrior and sometimes known as the Knight of the Dragon.

Sir Tom a'Lincoln

The illegitimate son of Arthur and Angelica, Tom a'Lincoln was also known as the Red Rose Knight. Made a commander of Arthur's army, he led a successful campaign against the Portuguese. He eloped with Anglitora,[19] but when she found out that he was illegitimate she murdered him. His death was eventually avenged by his son, one of the numerous Black Knights of Arthurian legend.

Sir Tor

The son of Pellinore who was made a Knight of the Round Table after he had killed a renegade knight, but was later killed by Sir Lancelot when that knight was carrying Guinevere off to safety. His brothers are named as the knights Aglovale, Perceval, Lamorak, Alan, Melodian, Driant and Dornar, and his sister as Elaine, the wife of Sir Miles.

Sir Turquine

The brother of Sir Carados, Turquine was a treacherous knight who wanted to kill Sir Lancelot in revenge for Lancelot's killing his brother, and he took Sir Ector de

Maris prisoner. Lancelot duly came to the rescue, killed Sir Turquine and released Ector de Maris and Turquine's other prisoners.

Sir Yder

A giant knight who fell in love with a maiden who said that she would marry him only if he brought her a knife that belonged to two giants. He accomplished the task and she kept her side of the bargain. Other sources say that Yder was a giant who did battle with three other giants at Brent Knoll in Somerset, but lost his life as a result.

It should be noted that these are not, by a long way, all the knights who have ever been connected with the Round Table. If they were all included, then this list would contain well over 200 names. One of the most complete lists compiled to date is given in *Warriors of Arthur* by John Matthews and Bob Stewart (see Further Reading, pages 186–8). This names 190 of Arthur's warriors and advisers, as well as 20 of the women of King Arthur's court.

No matter how many times the body of Arthurian literature, both ancient and modern, is studied, it is possible to add extra names to the list of knights who have, at some time and in the mind of one author or another, been Knights of the Round Table. Those who have been mentioned here, and those who are about to be profiled, have been chosen with great care, and all adhere to the simple rule that they appear in at least three of the ancient texts, whether by their Latinized name or by their Welsh, French, German or Italian variants.

PART TWO

The Heroes

King Arthur

THE SEMI-LEGENDARY, mythologized King of Britain was not always considered a member of the Round Table. However, as he instigated the order, he must have been numbered among that illustrious company. The origins of King Arthur have already been dealt with in Part One, but just what was the man really like?

Of course, there is no real answer to that question, and today we can only use our imagination to conjure up a picture. To do this with confidence we must first consider the immense pressure that the ancient Britons, the Celts, were under. They had already suffered long occupation by the Romans and, having survived that, now seemed to be on the very verge of extinction again at the hands of the Angles, the Saxons and the Jutes. Out of the gloom rose a man whose skill at fighting against overwhelming odds and emerging victorious shone like a beacon from the loftiest mountain.

This one man soon developed a cult following, along with an entourage who wished to be associated with him. Whether he actually welcomed the attentions of these 'disciples' is open to speculation, for even though many would have been worthy of association with him, there must have been those who simply wished to further their own ends by being seen in the company of just such a man – a human trait that is unfortunately as much in evidence today as it was then.

Quickly Arthur, for he has yet to be elevated to kingship, would have come to the attention of the local Celtic chiefs. His magnetism would have ensured that he rose quickly through the ranks, ending up as a general who could lead the Celtic forces into battle and emerge, more often than not, victorious. Evidence of this is to be found in the works of the Welsh writer Nennius (*fl.* 769), the author of the clumsily put together Latin *Historia Britonum*,[1] where he lists 12 battles in which

Arthur led the Britons to victory. Today it remains in doubt if any of these battles was actually associated with Arthur, but they all seem to have taken place and so it is logical to assume that Arthur played a role in all of them. He may well have led the Britons into battle at some, if not all, of them or his might have been the planning that led to the victories. One of the most fascinating things about the list given by Nennius is the sheer geographical diversity of the battles, from the south-west to the Lowlands of Scotland.[2]

Such diversity leads to the hypothesis that Arthur may have risen above the ranks of a general, the *dux bellorum* ('leader of battles') of Nennius, in his own lifetime, for to have such wide influence would seem to suggest that he held a position of authority almost across the length and breadth of Britain. Thus a man who quite obviously started life as a warrior became a king, the hero of his people and quite possibly a legend in his own lifetime. It is the legendary aspect, however, that draws us towards a quite different theory. Perhaps, due to his renown as a fighter, the Saxons were made to believe that Arthur would be leading the forces at each battle and this alone was sufficient to ensure a victory for the Celtic forces. Regrettably, we will never know, but it ensures that the legends that surround this enigmatic man remain some of the most popular, if perplexing, of all legends, European and Worldwide.

What started out life as an oral tradition – that is, passed down from father to son for generations – was seized upon by later writers, who elevated the fighting man into an almost godlike figure who could call upon magic to help him, as well as command respect from his peers. And yet these medieval writers seem to reverse the true potency of King Arthur, turning him into an almost quasi-tragic hero who did not always know his own mind and sometimes had to rely on others, when in fact those others would normally have relied on him. As the legends developed under the pens of successive writers, Arthur became a more pathetic and impotent figure who was finally destroyed by his own power, which he either failed to realize he wielded or used to ill effect. King Arthur can perhaps, best be summarized as a humble man who was elevated through his own prowess and man-management skills, but lost his way and was subsequently overwhelmed by the power that was his to use.

The earliest coherent narrative on the life of King Arthur as he is known today is to be found in the eleventh-century *Historia Regum Britanniae* (*History of the Kings of Britain*) by Geoffrey of Monmouth, a totally fictitious account of the pseudo-mythical history of Britain. Although worthless as history, it features a substantial Arthurian section. However, it was not until 1470, with the publication of *Le Morte d'Arthur* by Sir Thomas Malory (d. 1471), the fifteenth-century writer whose book is to this day regarded by many as the essential Arthuriad, that the story of Arthur as he is known now was first told. *Le Morte d'Arthur* remains the best prose romance in English and is an attempt by the writer to give epic unity to the whole mass of

Arthurian literature. It is the picture of King Arthur as conjured up by Malory that most people see when they talk about Arthur and his company of knights.

Arthur's story, drawn from a great number of sources, is basically as follows.

King Uther Pendragon[3] became infatuated with Igraine, the wife of Duke Gorlois of Cornwall, who had been waging a long war against the king, the war coming about, according to Geoffrey of Monmouth, when Gorlois, sensing the lust of Uther for his wife, left without taking the king's leave, a grave act of insubordination that was perceived as a challenge to the authority of the king. While Gorlois was besieged by Uther in Castle Terrabil, Igraine was in the castle at Tintagel,[4] but Uther could take no part in the fighting as he was sick with love for Igraine. One of his men (named by Geoffrey of Monmouth as Sir Ulfin de Ridcaradoch, who appears in no other sources) sought out the renowned wizard Merlin, who said he would help if the king would reward him with whatever he desired. Merlin required that any child born from the king's magical union be delivered to him to be raised, though Sir Thomas Malory says that the child should be delivered to Ector. Most commentators, however, agree that Ector fostered the child.

Merlin rode to Uther's pavilion, where the king agreed to Merlin's terms, and with the aid of his magic he so altered the king's appearance that when Uther came to her in her castle at Tintagel, Igraine believed him to be her husband. That very night, while the disguised king lay with Igraine, Gorlois was killed in battle with Uther's troops. When she heard of her husband's death, Igraine wondered about the identity of the knight who had lain with her. Even when she consented to marry Uther, to unite their two houses on the advice of his counsellors, he did not tell her. Their son, conceived on that night, was Arthur, brother to Morgan Le Fay, and, as Uther had been told, Merlin came to take the baby away, reassuring the father he would be well cared for.

Uther was unable to spend a long and happy life with Igraine, for within two years he had fallen sick and died, to the great sorrow of Igraine, who had learned to love him. The rule of the kingdom fell into jeopardy, for there was no known heir. Many lords laid claim to the throne and fought bitterly for the right to reign, but none could take the kingdom by just cause, a situation that was to remain for a further 13 years.

When Arthur was 15 he was chosen as king, the more romantic legends saying the choice was made by his drawing the magical sword Excalibur from a stone, something that no one else had been able to do. On this sword were engraved the words 'Whosoever shall draw this sword from the stone is the true born King of all England' or, alternatively, 'Whoso pulls this sword from the stone and anvil is rightwise King of all England.' The *Vulgate Version*[5] states that these words were inscribed in letters of gold on the stone itself and adds that the stone was more than that, being in fact a stone in which had been set an anvil through which the sword passed. Many maintain that this sword had been placed in the stone by Merlin, who 'arranged' that Arthur should be the only person capable of drawing it out, and that the sword was not Excalibur but one that had no special name. Others say that Merlin or Ector brought Arthur to London, where he won the kingship in a tournament. Still others combine both events, saying that Arthur drew the sword *en route* to the tournament (see profile for Sir Kay, pages 107–10).

The manner in which the sword Excalibur[6] came to King Arthur is quite widely covered, all sources tending to agree on how it came to be carried at his waist. Having fought and almost been killed by Sir Pellinore, during which fight Arthur broke the sword he had removed from the stone, Merlin took the youthful king to the shores of a vast lake and there told him that he would receive a sword he would thenceforth carry as a mark of his kingship and authority, for with it came the right to rule. Arthur was bemused to hear Merlin say that he would be offered the sword from the midst of a wide and very deep lake, but, as he always did in those early years, he trusted Merlin implicitly and so followed his adviser's instructions to the letter. As Arthur rowed out on to the lake, a hand lifted the sword out of the water and presented it in its scabbard to Arthur. Back on the shores of the lake, Merlin asked Arthur which he preferred, sword or scabbard. Arthur thought for a moment and then answered that he preferred the sword, at which Merlin chided him, saying that the scabbard was worth ten times the sword, for while Arthur carried the scabbard he would never lose any blood, no matter how badly wounded he was.

The crowning of Arthur led to a rebellion by 11 barons, which he successfully put down. It is interesting to note at this point that one of the leaders who rebelled against Arthur was Lot, the husband of Arthur's half-sister Morgause, the latter being sent by her husband to spy on Arthur. As each was unaware of their relationship, they had a brief affair, which led to the birth of the evil and scheming Sir Mordred. Lot was, as has already been shown (see pages 38–40), a major supplier of loyal and noble blood to the order of the Round Table, which seems surprising considering his original stance towards the young Arthur. Arthur then led an army against the Saxons and defeated their leader, Colgrin, and a mixed force of Saxons, Scots and Picts at the battle of the River Douglas in Linnius.[7] Colgrin took refuge in York, to which Arthur laid siege, but the king was obliged to abandon that siege and return to London. Now he sought the aid of Hoel, King of Brittany, his cousin (or possibly his nephew), who landed at Southampton with a great army. Together they defeated the Saxons at Lincoln, at Celidon Wood and at Bath, though it is quite possible that Hoel was present at all the battles listed by Nennius (see page 176). They put down the Scots, Picts and Irish in Moray, and toured Loch Lomond. Next they raised the siege of York, and Arthur restored that city to its former glory, returning their lands to three dispossessed Yorkist princes, Lot,[8] Urian[9] and Auguselus.[10]

Having now restored the entire kingdom, Arthur took as his wife the most beautiful woman in all Britain, Guinevere, the daughter of King Leodegrance of Cameliard, or the ward of Duke Cador, and a lady of noble Roman descent. Having married, Arthur sailed to Ireland, defeated its king, named by Geoffrey of Monmouth as the mythical Gilmaurius, and conquered the whole island. Hearing of his great might and prowess in battle, Doldavius and Gunphar, the Kings of Gotland and the Orkneys respectively, came to pay him homage. Now Arthur began to invite the most distinguished men of other lands to join his court and the fame of his knights spread to the ends of the earth.

The romances placed his court at Camelot, which has been variously identified, but the name is simply the invention of twelfth-century poets. Since at least 1540, Camelot has been identified with Cadbury Castle in Somerset.[11] Archaeological excavation, however, shows that Cadbury Castle might instead have been the stronghold or fortified rallying point that the historical Arthur needed to defend Britain against the Saxons. The hillfort was first constructed *c.*500 BC, but was refortified with a stone and timber rampart and gates that can be dated to between AD 460 and 540, the years during which Arthur is now thought to have flourished. Foundations of a large hall have been discovered, and the site, some 7 hectares (18 acres) in size, would have been large enough to accommodate an army of over 1,000 men. Early Welsh traditions named Arthur's court as Celliwig, and this is probably to be identified with Killibury or with Caerleon-on-Usk. Another tradition associated Arthur with Castle-an-Dinas near St Columb, the largest Celtic hillfort in Cornwall, which was also known as the seat of Cornish kings after Arthur's time.

His next expedition was to conquer Europe, beginning with Norway, which he duly vanquished and then gave to Lot, a gift that again seems surprising considering the antagonism between Arthur and Lot in the early days of Arthur's reign. Sailing then to Gaul, he defeated and killed the Tribune Frollo, who ruled Gaul for the Emperor Leo, and took Paris, where Frollo had originally taken refuge and outside which he was killed in single combat with the king. In nine years, with the aid of Hoel, Arthur had conquered all of Gaul and, holding court in Paris, he established the government of that kingdom on a legal footing. Returning to Britain, he decided to hold a plenary court at Whitsun at the City of the Legions (Caerleon-on-Usk or Chester), and to this court came representatives of all Europe to swear their allegiance to Arthur.

Arthur was now summoned to Rome by Lucius Hiberius[12] to answer the charge of having attacked the empire, and with 183,000 men Arthur crossed to France and marched southwards. *En route* he had a vision of a dragon fighting and conquering a bear, and decided that this represented his coming conflict with the emperor, though some of his company interpreted it as meaning that he would fight and overcome a giant. Indeed, at Mont-Saint-Michel, Arthur did defeat and kill a giant. He also routed the imperial Roman troops at Saussy, and was about to march on Rome when he received news that his nephew Mordred, son of Lot though actually his son by Morgause, whom he had left as his regent in Britain, had usurped the throne and taken Queen Guinevere as his mistress. Some accounts, however, say that Arthur successfully defeated Lucius Hiberius and became emperor himself.

The later romances treat this period in a different manner and include the most romantic knight of them all, Sir Lancelot.

Having achieved the quest for the Holy Grail, those knights who survived returned to Arthur's court and to the company of the Round Table. For a while it seemed as if the kingdom would be restored to its former glory, but Lancelot soon forgot his repentance and the vows he had made on the holy quest, and began to consort with Queen Guinevere again. Arthur was told of the affair, but refused to believe it unless Lancelot and his queen could be caught together.

Agravain and Mordred lay in wait with 12 other knights[13] and succeeded in trapping Lancelot in the queen's bedchamber. Even though Lancelot was unarmed, he managed to fight his way free, killing all who had sought to trap him except Mordred, who fled to the king. Guinevere was reluctantly sentenced by Arthur to burn at the stake. However, moments before the fire was lit, Lancelot rode into the throng that had gathered and rescued her, though in the process he killed a great number of his former colleagues, who were unarmed at the time. Lancelot and Guinevere then left Logres[14] for his lands in France. There is now some inconsistency in the romances, for even though Guinevere was supposed to be in France, the next part of the romances puts her back in Logres. In these cases, Guinevere was said to have been taken to Lancelot's castle, Joyous Gard, formerly called Dolorous Gard, which has been identified with Bamburgh Castle in Northumberland.

Arthur, who had earlier loved Lancelot and regarded him almost as his own son, or even brother, wanted nothing more than to go to France and compel Lancelot to return in peace, but upon taking the counsel of Gawain, who desired revenge for the killing of his brethren by Lancelot in his escape, or perhaps even through taking notice of what Sir Mordred said, Arthur was otherwise persuaded. Leaving Sir Mordred to rule in his absence, Arthur set sail for France, taking a vast army with him. The siege of Lancelot's castle wore on until Lancelot agreed to champion Guinevere in combat, and by so doing earned her a pardon and her freedom. She returned to England where she was placed under the governance of Mordred. Learning that the siege in France was likely to last for some considerable time, Mordred forged letters which he said had been sent from France. They told of Arthur's death in battle and, as he had been made regent by Arthur, he usurped the throne and had himself crowned king at Canterbury.

Next Mordred announced that he was going to marry Guinevere, and though the queen still mourned Arthur, she consented. Trusting her, Mordred gave Guinevere permission to travel to London to buy what she wanted for their wedding. Arriving in London, she went straight to the Tower of London,[15] which she stocked with provisions for a long siege. News of these events reached Arthur and he called back his troops.

Hurrying home, Arthur landed at Richborough, where he fought and defeated Mordred, though the latter did personally manage to dispose of Arthur's ally Auguselus during the battle. At the battle of Winchester, Arthur defeated Mordred again (the romances make this the site of Gawain's death), and then pursued him to the River Camlann in Cornwall, though the romances make this Salisbury Plain, the final battle to be fought on the day after Trinity Sunday. Cornish legend associates the battle of Camlann with Slaughterbridge, where the River Camel ran crimson with the blood of slain warriors[16].

In a dream, the spirit of Gawain appeared to Arthur and told him that if he were to fight the following day, both he and Mordred would be slain. However, if he waited, Sir Lancelot and all his noble knights would come to his aid within the month. Waking, Arthur called his two most trusted knights, the brothers Sir Bedivere and Sir Lucan, and charged them with making a truce with Mordred. All was agreed and both sides, with just 14 knights each, met on the field of combat to sign the treaty. Just then, an adder slithered from a bush and bit one of the knights on the foot. He drew his sword to kill the snake and the opposing armies, seeing the sword glinting in the sunlight, cried treachery and the battle began again.

Towards the end of the wholesale slaughter, King Arthur noticed Mordred leaning on his sword amidst a pile of bloody bodies. Grabbing a lance, he rushed his son and killed him with a single lunge. However, as Mordred fell to the ground, his sword struck Arthur a mortal blow. Sir Bedivere and Sir Lucan carried the dying king from the field of combat, the effort of doing so killing the badly wounded Lucan. Arthur then told Bedivere to take his enchanted sword, Excalibur, and throw it into a nearby lake.[17] Bedivere took the sword, but hid it behind a tree before returning to Arthur to tell him that his command had been carried out. However, when Arthur asked Bedivere what he had seen and Bedivere answered that he had seen nothing but waves and wind on the water, Arthur knew he was lying. He once more charged Bedivere to return to the lake and carry out his command. This time Bedivere, ashamed of what he had done, hurled the sword out over the lake and, as it fell towards the water, a hand clad in white or red samite rose and caught it. Returning to the king, Bedivere told him what he had seen.

Satisfied that his orders had been followed, Arthur told Bedivere to take him down to the water's edge, where a barge drew alongside. In the barge were a number of fair ladies, all with black hoods who wept as they saw Arthur. According to Geoffrey of Monmouth, these ladies were Morgan Le Fay, the chief of the nine *fays* or fairies who lived in the Otherworld realm of Avalon, six of her eight sisters being named as Moronoe, Mazoe, Gliten, Glitonea, Tyronoe and Thitis. Morgan Le Fay is, in this instance, not related to King Arthur but is described as the shape-changing mistress of therapy, music and the arts who could fly through the air on enchanted wings. Bedivere laid the weak king in the barge, which then sailed away from the site of the battle to the Isle of Avalon, Avallach or the vale of Avilion, so that his wounds might be healed. The barge was steered by Barinthus, a mysterious ancient Celtic sea or water deity, and the body of Arthur was accompanied by both Merlin and the magically conceived bard Taliesin. In the imagination of Alfred Lord Tennyson, the dying Arthur was carried down to the narrow harbour of Boscastle to be borne away on the funeral barge to Avalon. Before leaving, the king gave the crown to his cousin Constantine, son of Cador, Duke of Cornwall. This was reputed to be in the year 542, though, as has already been stated, no exact year for the battle of Camlann has been, or is ever likely to be, established.

According to Geoffrey of Monmouth, following Arthur's death, Guinevere fled to the abbey at Amesbury, where she took the veil and finally became the abbess. There she swooned when Lancelot came in search of her but, having taken her vows, she would not leave, so her lover travelled to Glastonbury, where he became a monk. Several years later, after her death, her body was taken to Glastonbury by Sir Lancelot to be buried beside that of her husband. Lancelot himself died there a short time later.

The belief that Arthur would return in the hour of Britain's greatest need and inaugurate a golden age was well established in both England and France by the early part of the twelfth century, and persisted until the end of the nineteenth century, although accounts of how and where the king would reappear varied considerably. In his twelfth-century *Vita Merlini*, Geoffrey of Monmouth had called Avalon the Isle of Apples, thus suggesting an Otherworldly realm that may have been cognate with the Irish Emhain Abhlach ('Emhain of the Apples'), but some 50 years later, in 1190 or 1191, Avalon had become identified with Glastonbury, where Arthur's body, together with Guinevere's, was said to have been exhumed, the inscription '*Hic jacet Arthurus, rex quondam, rexque futurus*' ('Here lies Arthur, King that was, King that shall be') summing up the flavour of his legendary life and death. All trace of the tombs mysteriously disappeared straight afterwards, but the claim attracted widespread interest at the time, when the tales of King Arthur were beginning to spread beyond purely Welsh legend. In other stories he is said to lie sleeping at Cadbury Castle in Somerset, in a cave on Craig-y-Dinas near Snowdon in Wales and even in another cave on Mount Etna, this last one probably deriving from the Norman occupation of Sicily.

So tenacious were the Cornish in their belief that Arthur would one day come again to rescue them from bondage that in 1177 there was a riot in Bodmin Church between local men and some visiting French monks, one of whom had scoffed at such an article of faith. Arthur's spirit was believed to fly over the Cornish cliffs in the form of the Cornish chough – a bird now extinct in the county except for one or two pairs held in captivity. His spirit is also said to have been reincarnated in a raven or a puffin – possibly because of the rarity of the chough.

In the later, medieval legends of King Arthur, which include the quest for the Holy Grail, that quest is undertaken by Sir Lancelot, Sir Galahad, Sir Perceval and Sir Bors, though most commentators agree that almost the entire company of the Knights of the Round Table would have undertaken this most holy of tasks.

Possibly the most mysterious aspect of Arthur's reign is his relationship with Morgan Le Fay. In Malory she is made his sister, but Geoffrey of Monmouth seems to know nothing of their kinship, nor does he, interestingly, mention any enmity between them. Instead he makes Morgan Le Fay the mistress of Avalon. The bad blood between Arthur and Morgan Le Fay would therefore appear to be a later development. One possible explanation is that Morgan Le Fay was originally Arthur's lover, later being represented as his sister. It is, however, generally accepted that Morgan Le Fay's enmity towards Arthur sprang from the fact that he killed her father, Gorlois, which would mean Morgan Le Fay was his half-sister, even though this account makes a mockery of the generally agreed scheme of things, in which Gorlois was killed on the very night Arthur was conceived. Arthur was also said by the different sources to have had many children, including the sons Loholt and Borre by either Guinevere or Lionors; Llacheu, who later became identified with Loholt; Arthur the Little, according to the *Prose Tristan*; Mordred by his half-sister Morgause, the wife of his once enemy Lot; Rowland, according to the Scottish ballad *Childe Rowland*; Gwydre, according to *Culhwch and Olwen*; Amr or Amhar, the former according to Nennius and the latter according to the *Mabinogion*; Adeluf and Patrick the Red, according to the *Petit Brut* of Rauf de Boun; Morgan the Red; Ilinot, according to Wolfram von Eschenbach; and the daughters Melora, according to Irish romance; Ellen, according to the Scottish *Childe Rowland*; and Gyneth by Gwendolen, according to the fairly modern work *Bridal of Triermain* (1813) by Sir Walter Scott.

Places linked with both the historical and the legendary Arthur are widespread throughout Britain, though most of the names connected with Arthur, King Mark and Tristan have no genuine historical significance. What they do show is a popular habit of naming ancient ruins after long-dead heroes. However, Cadbury Castle and Mote of Mark, a Cornish fortress, have both produced pottery that dates from the correct period, *c.*500, thus indicating that they may have some connection with the historical chieftain who became the most potent of all British, and indeed European, legendary figures, and who is better remembered, for example, than the Russian Ilya Muromyets, an enigmatic figure whose story is shrouded in such a tangle of history, myth and folklore that the truth will probably never be known.

Arthur's genealogy is particularly fascinating, simply for the pure scope and diversity of lineage, especially with regard to his parentage.

This should be compared with the family tree for the House of Lot (see page 39), as that shows a slightly altered descent for several of the characters in the legends, most notably the treacherous Sir Mordred.

The full genealogy of the *mythical* King Arthur – a point that is very important to stress, for no genealogy of the historical King Arthur is ever likely to be produced – is given opposite. This shows how many of the Knights of the Round Table were related by one means or another to their fellow knights. There are several important points to note from this genealogy. The first is that there is no ancestry shown for Gorlois, for nothing is actually known of his lineage. The second is the slightly strange arrangement of the ancestors of Igraine. Both lines of descent shown are Welsh in origin and both date from about the same period, but it is impossible to say which is correct, if indeed either of them is. The third point of specific interest concerns the children listed as having been King Arthur's progeny. None of those shown is directly attributed to his marriage with Guinevere and it seems quite likely that none of them actually was her child; rather they were the results of Arthur's philandering.

Geoffrey of Monmouth gives the following:

```
                        Constantine
                            |
              ┌─────────────┴──┐
          Ambrosius          Uther  =  Igraine  =  Gorlois
                            ┌───┴────┐
                          Arthur   Anna
```

Sir Thomas Malory gives:

```
                Uther   =   Igraine   =   Duke of Tintagel
                    |
 Guinevere = Arthur = Morgause = Lot    Morgan Le Fay = Urien   Elaine
              Mordred       Gawain                      Owain
                          & brothers
```

King Arthur's short family tree, allowing for inconsistencies, might resemble the following:

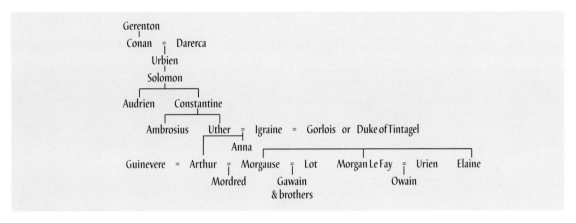

King Arthur's full genealogy is as follows:

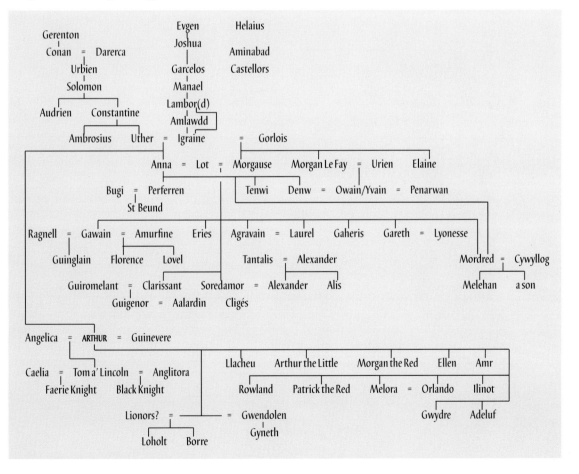

Sir Bedivere

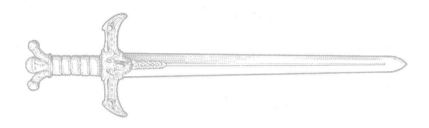

POSSIBLY ONE OF ARTHUR'S MOST LOYAL followers, Bedivere has his roots in Welsh legend, where he is named Bedwyr. The first references to a character of this name appear in the source texts that are combined within the nineteenth-century *Mabinogion*, and in particular in that part that relates the story of Culhwch and Olwen.

Bedwyr appears as a one-armed fighting man who, even though he is disabled, is still faster with the sword than three others fighting together. It seems quite remarkable that even 1,500 years or more ago a disabled man should find his way into the ancient legends, particularly as at that time anyone who was not physically perfect would have been scorned and derided. The truth behind the characterization of Bedwyr may lie in an adage that has survived until modern times. This says that a true hero may fight evil 'with one hand tied behind his back'. How many times do we today hear children boasting that they could beat someone in this manner, little realizing just how important just such a concept would have been to the ancient Britons? Bedwyr would therefore seem to be the embodiment of this concept, although rather than having his hand behind his back, he does not have it at all.

To understand the importance of Bedwyr to the ancient story, it is perhaps worth spending a few moments considering the full story as found in *Culhwch and Olwen*. Culhwch was the son of Kilydd and Goleuddydd, his mother being the sister of Arthur's mother, Igraine. During her pregnancy, Goleuddydd lost all reason and wandered aimlessly through the forests and mountains of Wales, living as a wild animal. However, her sanity returned in a rush as her labour pains started and, in the midst of a herd of swine, she gave birth to a boy. He was named Culhwch in honour of his birth-place, for *hwch* in Welsh means 'pig'.

Following the death of Goleuddydd, Culhwch's father, Kilydd, remarried, though for some reason the name of his new wife is not recorded. She appears to have been jealous of her stepson, perhaps as she did not have any children by Kilydd herself, for she placed Culhwch under an obligation to seek out and marry the maiden Olwen. Not a bad obligation to be placed under, or so you might think, until you learn that Olwen was the daughter of the *penkawr* or chief giant of Wales, a monstrous man by the name of Yspaddaden, who could never let his daughter marry, for if she did he would die.

Culhwch gladly accepted the task set him by his stepmother but, realizing the enormity of his quest, headed for the court of his cousin King Arthur to ask for help. He was met at the gates of the court, which here has no name, by Glewlwyd Gafaelfawr,[1] Arthur's gatekeeper, who took news of the stranger to the king, adding that never in his long and varied career had he seen such a handsome youth.

Admitted to the court, Culhwch was granted the boon he requested of King Arthur and a party was formed to help the young man seek out his bride. The party put together by Arthur included Cei (later to become Sir Kay), Bedwyr, Cynddylig, Gwrhyr, Gwalchmai (later to become Sir Gawain) and Menw fab Teirgwaedd. Each of the members of the party was chosen for his particular skill, though it is only that of Bedwyr, his ability to fight faster than three men with his single arm, that is of interest here.

The formation of a party to help Culhwch that included Bedwyr proves that the knight was already a member of King Arthur's court by that time. What it does not tell us is how he came to be counted among that august company. Supposition taking over, we must ask why a one-armed warrior should be accepted as part of the entourage of knights that surrounded the early, and indeed the later, King Arthur.

A modern parallel may be drawn from men who have lost limbs fighting for their country. Some of them are highly decorated on account of their valour. It is possible that Bedwyr too lost his arm doing some honourable deed, perhaps even protecting Arthur from a mythical beast or a hideous adversary, and was duly knighted as a reward. Alternatively, he may have lost his arm in a tournament but remained a knight, as it would have been considered unchivalrous to demote him after such an accident. This, of course, is pure speculation, for the truth has been long lost.

Bedwyr appears to have had amazing reflexes, for later in the story of Culhwch we learn that every time Yspaddaden fired a poisoned dart at Culhwch and his companions (some versions of the story say that Yspaddaden threw a poisoned boulder at the party), it was Bedwyr who caught it and threw it back, each time succeeding in hitting the giant, and after three days he had caused Yspaddaden such distress that he finally agreed to hear Culhwch's suit for the hand of his daughter. Though little more is heard of Bedwyr in the story of Culhwch, it would appear that he took part in many, if not all, of the tasks Yspaddaden set Culhwch before the latter could gain the hand of Olwen. These tasks were increasingly difficult, though with the help of his companions Culhwch managed to complete each and every one, only to have the giant set innumerable new terms and conditions. Finally, this became too much for Culhwch to stand and, with the help of his companions, he rounded up all of Yspaddaden's enemies, stormed the giant's castle and killed him.

When Bedwyr later resurfaced in the Latinized Arthurian legends, his name had become the more commonly known Bedivere, and he had his very own genealogy, which also calls his grandfather Bedivere, a relationship that has led some to speculate that Bedwyr from the early Welsh legends became Bedivere the grandfather of the Bedivere at King Arthur's court and that, as both had but a single arm, this was not due to some unfortunate accident but was rather a genetic trait. What this theory does not say is whether Pedrawt, Bedivere's father and thus the son of Bedwyr/Bedivere, had a single arm as well.

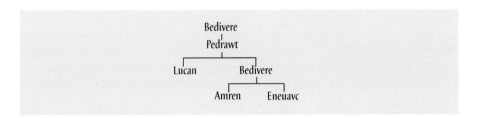

The stories of Bedivere after he became known by that name are a little confused, for, depending on which source is consulted, Bedivere either died during Arthur's campaign against Rome or survived the battle of Camlann and went on to become a hermit. The things that remain constant about are his lack of one arm, his great skill with the sword and his lightning-fast reflexes.

At the start of Arthur's campaign against the Roman Empire, the king and his knights were camped close to Mont-Saint-Michel in Brittany. While he slept, King Arthur dreamed of doing combat with a giant. The very next day the company travelled on to Mont-Saint-Michel and were there confronted by a monstrous being who quickly laid into King Arthur's knights. Bedivere's ability with the sword was to prove the deciding factor in the fight, for his great skill was put to good use in dispatching the giant. For this act, at least according to Geoffrey of Monmouth, Arthur made Bedivere the Duke of Neustria, but he later died during Arthur's battles against the might of the Roman Empire.

Sir Thomas Malory, however, has Bedivere survive both the Roman campaign and the subsequent siege of Sir Lancelot, and return to Britain when news of the treachery of Sir Mordred was brought to Arthur. He stood alongside the king at the first battle, fought at Richborough, and again at the second battle, at

Winchester. His location during the third and final battle, at Camlann, is unknown, but it has been suggested that he again stood by his monarch. He does, however, appear to have been one of the party accompanying Arthur to sign a truce shortly before the battle, although the truce was not signed because one of the knights there drew his sword to kill an adder and, amid shouts of 'Traitor', the battle recommenced.

Towards the end of the conflict, when hundreds lay dead all over the battlefield, the brothers Sir Lucan and Sir Bedivere were with King Arthur when the king sighted Mordred leaning on his sword among a pile of bodies. Calling for his lance, Arthur strode towards Mordred, even though both Lucan and Bedivere pleaded with him to let well alone, and Lucan himself was on the point of death from his own wounds. Arthur would hear none of it, for he now wanted the blood of his treacherous nephew, and, striding up to Mordred, he ran him through with his lance. As Mordred fell, he managed a last swipe with his sword and inflicted a mortal wound on the king. As Mordred fell dead, Lucan and Bedivere carried the dying king back to his pavilion.

There Sir Lucan was to die of his wounds, either from attempting to lift Arthur or from the strong embrace the king had given him. Alone, Sir Bedivere and King Arthur, the sole survivors of the battle of Camlann, surveyed the scenes of wholesale slaughter that surrounded them, and Arthur realized that his kingdom was no more, just as Merlin had foretold long ago.

Calling Sir Bedivere to his side, Arthur passed him Excalibur and told him to go to the nearby lake[2] and return the sword to whence it had come. Bedivere walked down to the shore of the lake, but rather than throw the sword into the water, he hid it behind a tree and went back to Arthur, telling him that his command had been carried out. Arthur asked Bedivere what he had seen, but when Bedivere answered that he had seen nought but the waves on the lake, Arthur immediately knew that Bedivere was lying. Again Arthur commanded Bedivere to cast Excalibur into the waters. Ashamed by his initial deceit, Bedivere took the sword from its hiding place and hurled it far out across the lake. As it fell towards the water, a hand clad in samite reached out and grasped it by its hilt before disappearing from view beneath the waves.

This time, when Bedivere told Arthur what he had seen, Arthur knew that his command had been carried out. Now Arthur had Sir Bedivere help him down to the shores of the lake, across which a thick mist had begun to spread. As Bedivere stood there helping to support King Arthur, a barge appeared, guided by a hooded steersman who is named as the ancient Celtic sea deity Barinthus in some sources. It glided to a rest beside the two warriors and Bedivere helped Arthur aboard. There he was made comfortable by Morgan Le Fay and her sisters. The barge, which was also said to have had Merlin and Taliesin on board, then moved off and Bedivere watched as it disappeared into the mist, taking Arthur to his final resting place in Avalon. For a long time Bedivere stood gazing into the distance before he turned and left, knowing for certain that his time as a Knight of the Round Table was at an end, as indeed was the very order itself, and that Britain would once more be plunged into the depths of despair.

As Bedivere walked among the dead on the battlefield of Camlann, he discarded his knightly clothes and laid down his sword. There, on bended knee, he swore never to raise arms against any man again, and duly ended his life as a hermit doing the work of God.

At the end Bedivere might appear to be a tragic figure, the sole survivor of the carnage of Camlann, but he is not to be pitied, for even though fate had decreed that he would lose an arm early in his career, he was the very embodiment of the medieval ideal. He overcame his disability to become a knight whom few, if any, could better, although he would have appeared a curious, lopsided figure in a one-armed suit of armour. His skill with the sword was unsurpassed, an amazing feat when the sheer size and weight of a medieval sword is taken into account. However, as Bedivere has his origins in the Welsh character Bedwyr, who dates from many centuries before the legends of King Arthur were romanticized, this feat may not have been as great, for the early Celtic swords of the fifth and sixth centuries were far shorter and lighter than their medieval counterparts. Even so, to wield a sword with only one arm and maintain balance would still have been a notable accomplishment, particularly as just such a one-armed man would have no means of holding a shield with which to parry blows.

The Black Knight

Possibly one of the most vivid images conjured up when we think of a tournament between two knights is that of the Black Knight, that dark, foreboding figure, dressed all in black, riding a magnificent black horse and usually fighting like the devil himself. The Black Knight is the essential representation of evil within the legends, whether Arthurian or from further afield. He is the dark child, usually born of a dark mother, whose powers are sometimes supernaturally enhanced.

The Black Knight possibly has his roots in the very earliest annals of man's history, at a time when it was far simpler to make a true division between good and evil, though these two concepts were not thought of individually but rather in unison, with one balancing the other. Therefore, when the early legends are examined and a black figure is encountered, there is usually a lighter figure in attendance.[1]

A good example is provided by the story of the Welsh hag Cerridwen, the wife of Tegid Voel. Cerridwen is the goddess of dark, prophetic powers whose totem animal, the sow, represents the fecundity of the Otherworld. She had two children, as would be expected of just such a goddess. Her daughter, Creirwy, was light and beautiful, while her son Morfran ab Tegid (see profile, pages 139–41), was dark and ugly.

Many Black Knights occur within the body of Arthurian legend. Some of them are by nature evil, but some are exactly the opposite. Perhaps one of the best known of all the good Black Knights is the son of Sir Tom a'Lincoln, whose family tree is illustrated on page 78.

This genealogy shows that Sir Tom a'Lincoln, one of the Knights of the Round Table, was the illegitimate son of King Arthur by Angelica. Raised by a shepherd,

```
                    Arthur  =  Angelica    Prester John
                             |                    |
          Caelia  =  Tom a' Lincoln  =  Anglitora
                  |                   |
          The Faerie Knight    The Black Knight
```

Tom a'Lincoln was knighted by Arthur when he came of age and given the position of a commander in Arthur's army, in which capacity he was said to have successfully defeated the Portuguese. Tom a'Lincoln, whom some say was born in the city of Lincoln, from where his mother came, then travelled to the realm of the mythical Prester John, who was alleged to have ruled in either Asia or Africa, and eloped with his daughter Anglitora, who later bore him a son, whose true name remains a mystery, for he is only ever referred to in legends as the Black Knight.

Prior to this, Tom a'Lincoln had had a brief tryst with a fairy lover by the name of Caelia, their son by this union appropriately being known as the Faerie Knight. This fact alone signifies that this particular Black Knight might originally have been perceived as an evil knight, for the Faerie Knight would then have been his contrast, a good knight who appeared in the legends dressed in light coloured armour.

All seemed well between Anglitora and Tom a'Lincoln until she discovered that he was illegitimate, whereupon she deserted him and became the mistress of an unnamed lord. Tom a'Lincoln went in search of her and Anglitora murdered him. News of his death reached his son, some sources claiming that the ghost of his dead father appeared to him, and he travelled to the castle where Anglitora was living, defeated the lord of the castle and then avenged his father's death by killing Anglitora. The Black Knight then met up with the Faerie Knight and the two became travelling companions, eventually arriving in England, though the legends do not tell us if they became Knights of the Round Table. It seems quite likely that they did, particularly as this Black Knight would have been King Arthur's grandson. In this instance perhaps the knight took to wearing black only after the death of his father, and thus the colour marks his mourning. It might also be taken as a sign of his wisdom or of his Christianity. Unfortunately, the truth will never be known, as the legends tell us little more about this Black Knight.

Another good Black Knight was Sir Breunor, the brother of Dinadan, who arrived at King Arthur's court wearing such an ill-fitting coat that it quickly earned him the nickname La Cote Male Tailée ('The Badly Cut Coat'). Some sources say that the ever impertinent Sir Kay was the originator of this appellation. Sir Breunor refused to remove the coat until he had avenged the death of his father, though the legends tell us neither how his father was killed nor whether Sir Breunor ever did exact his revenge.

Shortly after Sir Breunor's arrival at Camelot, the maiden Maledisant came to seek Arthur's help. Sir Breunor was dispatched to champion the maiden's cause, but she cruelly derided him, presumably because of his badly fitting garb, until he had proved his worth, which he obviously did, for he subsequently married Maledisant and became the master of Pendragon Castle, though exactly where this castle was located is never revealed in the legends.

There are several other good Black Knights within the Arthurian legends, but all of them appear only in fleeting references. One was the son of the King of the Carlachs.[2] He was defeated in combat by the Knight of the Lantern, the son of Libearn, the two combatants possibly being yet another instance of light and dark, for the Knight of the Lantern, a name that portrays lightness admirably, is also described as the son of the King of the Carlachs, to whom his mother was married or with whom she had had an affair. Another was a knight who discovered that his wife had exchanged a ring, in all innocence, with Sir Perceval. Swearing his revenge, this Black Knight bound his wife to a tree and awaited the arrival of Sir Perceval, who duly came, defeated the Black Knight and released the unfortunate lady. The truth behind the matter was then revealed and the Black Knight and his wife were reconciled. Again, this story reflects the opposing forces in play, for Perceval represents the light and the Black Knight the dark.

Evil Black Knights seem to appear in almost every story, but they are almost always defeated with relative ease by good knights, whether Red, Green or indeed any other colour, for all the colours of the spectrum appear at some point within the legends. The most famous evil Black Knight of all is perhaps Sir Mordred, who is profiled later (see pages 135–7).

However, another equally famous evil Black Knight is the one who helped a Red Knight to lay siege to the lady Lyonesse. This knight, whose true name was Sir Percard, was seeking to further his status when, or if, his master, Sir Ironside, the Red Knight of the Red Lands, married Lyonesse and thus became master of all her lands. Lyonesse dispatched her sister Lynette to ask help of King Arthur, who sent Sir Gareth (see profile, pages 93–9).

Having arrived at the realm of Lyonesse, Gareth first defeated a Green Knight before coming up against the Black Knight, whom he knocked to the ground during their joust. As the Black Knight rose to his knees, Sir Gareth sheathed his sword and spared his life, a mark of true chivalry. This Black Knight, Sir Percard, became a reformed character, as well as one of the Knights of the Round Table.

There is little evidence to support the idea that Black Knights actually existed during the reign of the historical King Arthur. They owe their origin to the furtive minds of the medieval writers who sought to conjure up such a strong image that there could be no mistake – a Black Knight was an evil knight. Yet, as has been shown, this was not always the case, for in history we have examples of Black Knights who were anything but evil. The most famous historical Black Knight must surely be the Black Prince, Edward (1330–76), Prince of Wales, the oldest son of King Edward III, who appears to have worn his black armour to frighten his enemies – wherein might lie the truth behind the legendary characters.

Sir Bors

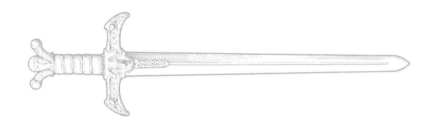

APPARENTLY OWING HIS ORIGIN to the Welsh character Gwri, one of the Twenty-four Knights of King Arthur's Court, Sir Bors is described as chaste, a quality that a great many of his fellow knights did not share. He was seen by the medieval writers as the epitome of virtue, though even they could not resist, when writing about the quest for the Holy Grail, to sully his character just a little, for even though he was embarked on that great adventure, he was not considered pure enough to fully achieve the Grail itself.

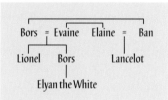

Medieval writers give Sir Bors the short geneology shown right.

It is the second Bors in this genealogy who is of concern here. His father was the brother of Ban, King of Brittany, and himself the King of Gaul or Gannes, thus suggesting that his brother was actually a vassal king. The younger Bors was raised by Pharien after his father had died and his mother, Evaine, had taken the veil, becoming a nun. Pharien, however, soon passed Bors and his brother Lionel into the care of Claudas,[1] Pharien's lover and one-time opponent of the elder Bors. Bors and Lionel, realizing that their lives were in danger, made good their escape from the hands of Claudas by changing themselves into greyhounds,[2] but they killed Claudas's son Dorin, who sought to stop them.

Bors and Lionel crossed the English Channel and made their way to King Arthur's court, where they were welcomed warmly to the order of Knights of the Round Table. After Arthur had defeated Claudas during his Continental campaign, he offered the throne of Gaul to Bors, but as Bors preferred to stay in England, Arthur installed his brother instead. Bors, meanwhile, had come to the attention of an unnamed daughter of King Brandegoris, the ruler of Stranggore,[3] and one of the 11 leaders who had rebelled against the youthful King Arthur, but he would have nothing to do with her. With the aid of her nurse, who presented Bors with an enchanted ring, the daughter forced Bors to sleep with her. The son who resulted from that union, Elyan the White, eventually became the Emperor of Constantinople, though during the traditional Arthurian period Constantinople was called Byzantium and was the capital of the Eastern Roman Empire.

Through the birth of an illegitimate child the medieval writers ensured that Sir Bors would not be entirely successful when he embarked, along with a great number of his comrades, on the quest for the Holy Grail. His involvement in the quest was as follows.

Bors departed from Camelot in the company of Sir Perceval and Sir Galahad, though at one stage he found himself separated from his companions and it was on this occasion that he met an anchorite (a religious hermit), riding on an ass. Bors saluted the man, who inquired as to Sir Bors's name and purpose. When he found out that Sir Bors was one of the knights involved in the quest for the Holy Grail, he told him that the Grail would be achieved only by Christian belief and the confession of sins.

Sir Bors accompanied the man to his hermitage, which they entered together. Inside, Sir Bors made a full confession of his sins before sitting down to eat the humble fare of the hermit. The hermit then instructed Sir Bors that he should not eat again until he was sitting at the table where the Holy Grail was. Sir Bors readily agreed, accepting that the hermit knew he would be among the knights who were to see the holy vessel. The hermit also told Sir Bors to remove his armour and gave him a simple coat of red to wear, again instructing him not to remove it until he had been in the presence of the Grail. Wearing the red coat and taking only his sword and shield with him, Sir Bors left the hermitage.

As he travelled he often thought of the words of the hermit, and by so doing saved himself from sinning on a number of occasions. However, once Sir Bors could do nothing but fight, even though he was unwittingly being challenged by his brother Sir Lionel, neither party recognizing the other, perhaps because of the simple garb Bors now wore. Just as Sir Bors gained the upper hand and raised his sword to deal a mortal blow to his brother, a voice cried out that he should do him no harm. As Sir Bors sheathed his sword, a ball of fire appeared between the brothers which burned both knights' shields to cinders and left the men unconscious. When Sir Bors came around he finally recognized his brother and begged his forgiveness, which Sir Lionel gladly granted.

As Sir Lionel bade his brother farewell, the mysterious voice returned and told Sir Bors to ride straight for the sea to find Sir Perceval, who awaited him. Sir Bors rode as quickly as he could until he came to the strand (the poetic term used widely throughout the Arthurian legends to refer to a beach or the sea-shore), where he found a vessel covered in white samite which, as soon as he stepped aboard, set sail so quickly that it appeared to be flying over the waves. Sir Bors, wearied from his exploits, lay down and slept until the following morning when he awoke to find a knight asleep in the middle of the vessel. As that knight awoke they recognized each other, for the knight was none other than Sir Perceval. Together they sailed on until the little craft reached a distant shore, where they were joined by Sir Galahad, and the three continued their quest together.

They rode hard until they reached Castle Carbonek, where they were greeted cordially by King Pelles,[4] who knew that the quest for the Holy Grail would now be achieved. That evening, King Pelles, his son Eliazar and the three knights sat down to dine, but before they could eat a voice was heard to say: 'There are two among you that are not in the quest for the Holy Grail, and therefore you both should depart.' King Pelles and his son stood up and slipped away. As soon as they had gone, a man and four angels appeared in the hall. The angels set the man down before a silver table and on that table the Holy Grail appeared. The man, dressed in the robes of a bishop, then started to celebrate Mass before kissing Sir Galahad and instructing that knight to kiss both of his companions. As Sir Galahad carried out the request, the man disappeared.

Now the three knights watched as a man with freely bleeding wounds appeared out of the Grail. He offered the Grail to Sir Galahad and then told him that he and his companions should depart the following day in a boat they would find ready and waiting for them. The next morning, the three knights set out from Castle Carbonek and after three days came to a small ship, on board which they found a silver table and the Holy Grail covered in a cloth of red samite. As they knelt to pray, the ship slipped its moorings and carried them to the pagan city of Sarras, where they disembarked and took the silver table with them. They stayed in Sarras for 12 months, though some sources make this a period of imprisonment, before a man in the likeness of a bishop came to them with the Holy Grail. Together they celebrated Mass, after which the man revealed his identity as Joseph, the son of Joseph of Arimathea. Sir Galahad, knowing now that his time on earth was at an end, knelt before the table and quietly passed away.

Sir Perceval and Sir Bors watched as a host of angels bore the body of Sir Galahad away, along with the Holy Grail, before they set out to return to King Arthur's court. There they were greeted with great warmth, though sadness hung in the air, for the Knights of the Round Table had been seriously depleted by the quest. (The full story of the quest for the Holy Grail will be found in the profile of Sir Galahad, see pages 87–9.)

All was well at the court until an unfortunate incident when Sir Pinel tried to poison Sir Gawain, but mistakenly poisoned Sir Petroc, whom some legends also call Sir Patrise or Sir Patrick. This would not have been a notable event had not the apple that killed Sir Petroc been brought to the table by Guinevere (Pinel had subsequently poisoned it) and the blame quickly fell upon the queen when Sir Mador, knowing that the fruit had been brought to the table by Guinevere, accused her of murder. The hapless Guinevere was reluctant to defend herself, as this would bring shame on the Round Table, and Sir Mador charged Arthur with naming a date for the combat that would prove the queen's guilt.

At first reluctant, Arthur finally agreed to set a date after he had been derided for not upholding the laws of knighthood, as he would expect the other knights present to do. Arthur's reluctance was furthered when all the knights feasting that day refused to champion Guinevere. Arthur decreed that the combat should take place 15 days hence at Westminster, and that if a knight could be found to champion the cause of Guinevere, then God would decide, but if not then Guinevere would be burned at the stake.

That night, upon the advice of Arthur, Guinevere sent for Sir Bors and requested that he should champion her. Sir Bors, however, refused, since he was honour bound by his oath at the Round Table not to meddle in the affair, for to do so would also incriminate him. At that, Guinevere dropped to her knees and begged him to do battle in her name, otherwise she would die undeservedly at the stake. At this point King Arthur walked into the room just as Sir Bors was pulling Guinevere back to her feet and chiding her for doing him a dishonour.

Arthur, seeing that Bors had refused his queen, asked the knight himself to do battle for the honour of his wife, whom he knew to be innocent. Though this meant that Bors would be outcast by the other members of the Round Table, his ethics told him that he had no option other than to stand for Guinevere in the combat. That night he rode to the hermitage of Sir Brastias, where he knew Sir Lancelot was staying, and told him all that had happened. Lancelot told Sir Bors to make ready for the combat, but to attempt to delay the actual fight until he could arrive.

Sir Bors duly rode back to Camelot and made ready to do combat with Sir Mador, knowing, or rather hoping, that Sir Lancelot would arrive in time and win the day for his queen. At the start of the combat, the two knights took their positions at either end of the jousting run. Moments before it was due to commence, a knight in gleaming armour appeared out of the woods and discharged Sir Bors of his obligation, taking his place instead, all the time hiding his true identity. The combat was fought hard and long until, though badly wounded himself, the mysterious knight had Sir Mador at his disposal. He then spared him once he had sworn that he had slandered the queen and would never repeat the false allegations of murder.

Guinevere was totally acquitted of the charges Sir Mador had brought against her and Sir Bors was thanked for his part in things. It was only at this point that Sir Lancelot revealed his identity and was welcomed back to the court of King Arthur.

Sir Bors was later to prove his allegiance to Queen Guinevere again after the abortive attempt of Sir Mordred, Sir Agravain and 12 other knights to trap Sir

Lancelot in the bedchamber of the queen, for Sir Bors helped Guinevere to escape from Camelot, though he hurriedly rushed back to the court in an attempt to put down the rebellion being fomented by Sir Mordred. How successful he was is unrecorded, but he appears to have remained loyal to both King Arthur and Queen Guinevere until the very end, though his conflict over his cousin Lancelot must have, been unbearable at times. A number of sources say that Sir Bors survived the battle of Camlann and was eventually to die on one of the Crusades, though which one is not known.

The characterization of Sir Bors is a little curious. He was loyal to both king and queen, but also to his cousin. He is perhaps best summed up as a career knight, bound by the laws and ethics of chivalry, who always did his best but by doing so continually found himself pulled in many different directions. One can only imagine how he must have felt when his cousin Lancelot was forced to flee after having been caught with Guinevere. On the one hand, he would have felt obliged to stand by his cousin and the queen, and yet just as strongly he would have felt honour bound to stand by his king. The conflict must have been staggering and yet the legends portray Sir Bors as a gentle knight who was seldom ruffled, and because of his honesty, both in what he thought and in what he did, the medieval writers rewarded him by letting him achieve the Holy Grail.

Sir Galahad

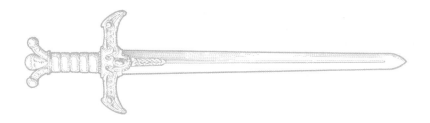

THE GRANDSON OF BAN and the natural son of Lancelot whose mother is variously given as Elaine, Amite or Perevida, the first being the most common. Possibly simply the creation of the author of the thirteenth-century French romance *Queste del Sainte Graal*,[1] as this is where he first appears, he may also be derived from the Palestinian place name Gilead, which appears widely in the Holy Bible, or from the Welsh character of Gwalhafed, who is mentioned in the *Mabinogion* book of *Culhwch and Olwen*. It has even been suggested that he derives from St Illtyd, possibly being that saint's son. Sir Galahad is always, without exception, portrayed as the ultimate ideal of a pure, chaste and chivalrous knight.

As a child he was placed in a nunnery, where his paternal great-aunt was the abbess, later being knighted there by his father, Lancelot, although at this stage it appears that Sir Lancelot did not recognize his son. His story is almost entirely concerned with the quest for the Holy Grail and is, basically, as follows.

One day a sword in a marble and iron stone was spotted in a river by a company of Arthur's knights and taken back to Camelot, this event occurring shortly before the feast of Pentecost,[2] when it was the custom of the Knights of the Round Table to gather and exchange stories of their exploits, as well as to reaffirm their allegiance to both King Arthur and the order to which they belonged. That year, the knights found that one of the sieges, or seats, at the Round Table now held the words 'Four hundred winters and four and fifty after the passion of our Lord Jesu Christ ought this siege to be fulfilled' — that is, *c*.490 AD.

Sir Lancelot calculated that the siege ought to be filled that very day. All the other knights present agreed and covered the siege, known as the Siege Perilous,[3] with a silk cloth so that the holy words could not be seen until the rightful knight came into their midst. They did not have to wait long. As each knight took his place at the Round Table an old man entered in the company of a fresh-faced young knight whose only armament was an empty scabbard at his waist. As the entire company watched, the old man led the boy up to the Round Table and then to the Siege Perilous, beside Sir Lancelot. Lifting the silk cloth from the seat, the gathered knights saw that the wording had changed and now read 'This is the siege of Galahad the haut prince'. The old man then seated the young man on the Siege Perilous and departed. Of the knights there present, only Sir Lancelot realized that all that had been prophesied had been fulfilled by his son.

The next day Galahad was taken to where the sword in the stone had been placed, though some accounts say that this was still where it had been found, rather than the entire object having been carried into Camelot. Arthur bade many of his knights to try to remove the sword, but all failed. Only one, Sir Lancelot, refused to try, for on the sword was a legend stating that only the best knight in all the world should pull it clear, and as he had sinned through his love for Guinevere, he could not consider himself worthy even to try. Finally Arthur put forward Galahad who easily withdrew the sword, which was a perfect fit for the empty scabbard at his side.

At a great jousting tournament subsequently arranged so that Galahad might test his skills against the other knights, he acquitted himself superbly, managing to unseat a good many of the Knights of the Round Table, save two who did not do combat that day, Sir Lancelot and Sir Perceval. That evening, as the knights once more gathered at the Round Table, they had scarcely sat down when there was a monstrous roll of thunder that shook the very walls. Amidst this clamour a brilliant light appeared and flooded the hall, this light being described as 'seven times clearer' than daylight. All the knights felt elated, as they were filled with the grace of the Holy Ghost.[4]

Then a golden centre appeared in this light, and when the knights became accustomed to the brilliance of this new and even brighter light, they saw a vessel, covered in white samite. This was the Holy Grail and with it came all manner of meat and drink that the knights loved best. Slowly the Grail crossed the hall and then vanished as quickly as it had appeared. In the sudden emptiness of the hall, the entire company began to speak at once.

Sir Gawain was the first to his feet and pledged that he would go out on a quest for the Holy Grail, promising to labour 'for a year and a day, or longer if need be', not resting until he had seen the Grail more openly than he had that night. One by one, all the knights present made the same pledge, but Arthur remained silent, for he remembered the prophecies of Merlin, and knew that many of his knights, his friends, would never return and never again would the Round Table be complete. Before he left Sir Galahad was given a white shield that had been made by Evelake[5] and that had a red cross on it that had been painted in blood by Joseph of Arimathea.

After about a year of fruitless questing, Sir Galahad came to a hermitage where he sought lodgings for the night. While he slept there, a lady came and asked the hermit if she might speak with the weary Sir Galahad. She told Galahad to arm himself and follow her, for she would show him an adventure the like of which no other knight would ever know. Three days later the pair came to the sea, where they found the ship of Sir Bors and Sir Perceval. Dismounting, they left their horses on the beach and took only their saddles and bridles on to the ship, where Sir Galahad was greeted with warmth and affection by his comrades.

The ship set sail and after a long time came to a strange land, the entrance to which was between two rocks with a whirlpool in between. Leaving their ship outside the entrance, the three knights and the lady transferred to another boat that was lying there, which bore a legend stating that only faith would see them safely through. The lady then turned to Sir Perceval and asked him if he knew her. Perceval replied that he did not, whereupon she revealed that she was his sister Dindrane,[5] and that she knew his faith would be sufficient to see them through.

As she spoke, the small boat sailed easily between the two rocks and came to land. Before disembarking, Sir Galahad found a sword lying in the middle of the ship, along with a crown. Both Sir Perceval and Sir Bors attempted to take the sword but found they were unable to draw it from its scabbard. Next Sir Galahad stepped forward, but he saw words written in blood on the sword saying that its owner would never die from loss of blood. Sir Galahad turned to his companions and refused to take the sword, for he felt that to do so would be a sin for which there could be no forgiveness. However, Dindrane told him that the sword, which had once belonged to the biblical King David, was his and his alone, for no other knight in the world would ever be able to own it.[6]

Sir Galahad stepped forward and drew the sword, which was more wondrous to behold than even Excalibur itself. Shortly afterwards the three knights and Dindrane left the ship and continued their quest, during which time they came across a castle where the mistress had been stricken with leprosy. Dindrane offered her own life in exchange and died when giving her blood to the mistress of the castle. Following her last instructions, the three knights laid her body back in the boat that had brought them to that land and set it adrift with a note explaining how and why Dindrane had died. It is possible that Sir Galahad here replaced hangings for the sword of King David with some made from the hair of Dindrane.

The three knights then parted company and for a while Galahad journeyed alone, until he once again came across the boat within which lay Dindrane's body. She, however, was no longer alone, for she was now accompanied by Sir Lancelot. For six months, father and son travelled together, visiting Evelake (who afterwards died) and regaling each other with their adventures, until finally Galahad was called away from his father to return to the quest that it had been ordained he would achieve. Having parted from his father, Galahad once again joined up with Sir

Perceval and Sir Bors. These three knights finally came to Castle Carbonek (also called Corbenic Castle), the Grail Castle, where they were greeted and entertained cordially by King Pelles and his son, Eliazer, something that is not altogether surprising as Pelles was the grandfather of Sir Galahad, whose mother, in most versions, was his daughter Elaine. That evening, as the five men sat down to dine, a voice came to them and told them that two there present were not to achieve the Grail and should leave immediately. Pelles and Eliazer quickly slipped away. No sooner had they departed than four angels appeared carrying a man whom they set down before a silver table, and on that table the Holy Grail appeared. The man, who was none other than Joseph of Arimathea, was dressed in the robes of a bishop and started to celebrate Mass. He kissed Galahad and told him to kiss his fellow knights, which he did. Joseph of Arimathea then vanished.

Watching the Grail, the three knights saw a man appear from within it, a man who had the freely bleeding wounds of Jesus Christ. This man offered the Holy Grail to Sir Galahad, who knelt and received the blessing of his Saviour. Galahad, Bors and Perceval were then told that they must depart the following day and put to sea in a boat they would find waiting for them.

Before leaving, Galahad anointed the Maimed King (Pelles) with blood from the Grail Spear, thus curing him of the injury that he had received as a divine punishment. Having left Castle Carbonek, the three knights travelled for three days before they came to a ship, on board which they once again found the table of silver and the Holy Grail, and in this vessel they sailed to the pagan city of Sarras. There the king, Estorause,[7] cast them into a prison, where they were sustained by the Grail, though some say that the three knights stayed in Sarras of their own free will. As Estorause lay dying, the three gallant knights forgave him for having imprisoned them and, following his death, Galahad became the new king of Sarras.

One year later the Holy Grail once more appeared to the three knights, this time in the company of Joseph, the son of Joseph of Arimathea. Galahad duly celebrated Mass and, having done so, asked that he should be allowed to die, which he did in peace. As Sir Bors and Sir Perceval watched, a host of angels came down from heaven and bore the body of Sir Galahad, along with the Holy Grail, to heaven.

Various commentators have given Galahad any number of lines of descent. However, that most widely accepted is shown here. In this it should be noted that the first Lancelot is not the famous Sir Lancelot but rather has been equated with the Sir Galahad who features amongst the Twenty-four Knights of King Arthur's Court as listed in the *Pedwar Marchog ar Hugan Llys Arthur*.

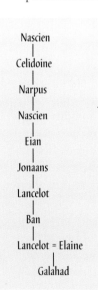

Nascien
|
Celidoine
|
Narpus
|
Nascien
|
Eian
|
Jonaans
|
Lancelot
|
Ban
|
Lancelot = Elaine
|
Galahad

Sir Galahad was the purest of knights, though his birth would do little to suggest that this was the case, for he was an illegitimate son born out of the lust of his mother for Sir Lancelot. And yet the medieval writers dealt with this very cunningly by saying that the event was planned to fulfil what had already been ordained, though by whom they omit to tell us.

Sir Gareth

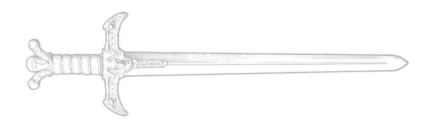

THE STORY OF SIR GARETH is first recounted by Sir Thomas Malory. However, it has a decidedly French flavour and is quite possibly based on a now-lost French romance.

A son of Lot and Morgause, and thus related to King Arthur, Gareth came to Arthur's court in disguise during a Whitsuntide feast,[1] unwilling or unable to reveal his true identity. He is described as a handsome young man, wide in the chest and large handed, and taller than any of the Knights of the Round Table by about one cubit – an ancient measure of length based on the forearm. Having arrived at court, Gareth was beckoned by King Arthur to come to his table, where the king greeted him warmly. Gareth replied by asking Arthur to grant him three boons, the first of which was to give him food and drink for a period of twelve months. Arthur readily agreed and passed him into the care of his steward, Sir Kay.

Sir Kay looked at the young man in disgust and, thinking about how to deal with this newcomer, quickly assigned him to the castle kitchens, there to live and work for the next 12 months. Sir Kay also gave the unnamed youth a name of his own, the nickname Beaumains – 'Fair Hands' – indicating that his hands were unsullied and unused to hard work. For the entire year Gareth lived and worked in the kitchens, never grumbling once and always treating everyone with the same level of respect, whether they be knight or commoner. Not all the knights, however, treated him with the disdain of Sir Kay, for they recognized that the youth had enormous potential. Two in particular, Sir Lancelot and Sir Gawain, always treated him as their equal, gave him money to spend and clothes to wear, and always asked him to participate in their games.

A year passed and once again King Arthur held a great feast at Whitsuntide. A fair maiden arrived at the court during the course of the feast and was admitted to ask for King Arthur's help on behalf of her sister, who was being besieged by a tyrant knight. Arthur asked her to reveal the name of her sister, but she refused, adding only that she was exceedingly beautiful and was under siege from the Red Knight of the Red Lands, Sir Ironside. Hearing this, Sir Gawain leapt to his feet and told the entire company that he had heard of this knight, adding that he was said to be as strong as seven normal men, and that when he had done combat with him he had been lucky to escape with his life.

However, Arthur would not dispatch a knight from his court to help the maiden in distress if her name was not revealed. At this point Gareth approached the king and asked for his remaining two boons to be granted. The first was to undertake the adventure being offered by the maiden in distress. The second was to be knighted by Sir Lancelot, for Gareth would accept that honour from no one else. Both were immediately granted, but the maiden turned in anger and chided the king for granting her the help of a mere kitchenhand. As she stormed out of the great hall, muttering to herself, a page approached and told Gareth that a dwarf had arrived at the gates of the court with all the apparel a knight would ever need. Once properly attired, Gareth left and hurried after the maiden, who had ridden away in disgust.

As Gareth left the court, Sir Kay rose to his feet and told the entire company that he would go after Beaumains – for his name was still unknown at court – and challenge him. Both Sir Lancelot and Sir Gawain told him to leave Gareth alone, but Sir Kay laughed and rode off after him, coming upon him just as he had caught up with the maiden. However, all did not go as Sir Kay had planned for, when he charged Gareth, that knight severely wounded him before stripping him of his armour, sword and shield and telling the dwarf who had accompanied him to take Sir Kay's horse. All this had been seen by Sir Lancelot who had followed Sir Kay, and it was now his turn to do combat with Gareth, though Gareth first asked Sir Lancelot for the honour of entering into combat with him.

Sir Lancelot agreed and the pair rode hard at each other, knocking each other to the ground. Lancelot was the first to rise and he helped Gareth to his feet. The pair then fought on foot for over an hour, until they laid down their weapons and sat panting heavily on the ground, each congratulating the other for his prowess, though secretly Lancelot was glad not to have come off the worse, like Sir Kay. Sitting on the ground, Sir Lancelot asked Sir Gareth to reveal his identity, but Gareth would do so only after Sir Lancelot had promised not to tell anyone his name until after it was openly known. He agreed, and in a clearing in the forest Sir Lancelot knighted Gareth. Sir Lancelot then left Sir Gareth, returned to where Kay still lay and had some men carry that sorry knight back to Arthur's court for his wounds to be healed.

Sir Gareth rode hard until he had once again caught up with the maiden, but she would have little or nothing to do with him. She continually sneered at him, complained that he still smelt of the kitchens, and made little or nothing of the fact that he had soundly beaten Sir Kay and had stood his ground against the might of Sir Lancelot. They rode on for many hours, the maiden letting loose an almost continuous stream of abuse, but never once did Gareth make any retort. He simply continued in silence.

Just after they had entered some woods, they came across a man riding like the wind who told them that his master was being set upon by six thieves. Without hesitation, Gareth rode off and quickly killed three of the thieves, the other three fleeing from the fight but with Gareth in hot pursuit. With the knight bearing down on them, the three thieves turned and fought, but one by one they fell to Gareth, who then returned to where the thieves had tied the knight to a tree. The knight thanked Sir Gareth and, as night was fast approaching, asked them to lodge with him in his castle, but once inside the maiden made such a fuss that a scullion (an archaic term for a servant hired to work in the kitchens; it can also mean a mean or despicable person, and as such might be applied to Sir Kay) had been seated in precedence to her that the knight moved Sir Gareth to a side table and seated the maiden at the top table.

The following morning Sir Gareth and the maiden bade farewell to the knight and continued on their journey, the maiden still pouring scorn on Sir Gareth, saying that she remained unimpressed by him. They rode on until they came to a river across which two knights sat, ready for combat. Without a word, Sir Gareth charged into the water, as did one of the two knights. After a long fight, Sir Gareth unseated his opponent, before leaving the river to do combat with the other knight. Again the fight was long and hard, but finally Sir Gareth split the knight's helmet in two.

As they rode away the maiden started her abuse of Sir Gareth again, saying that the first knight's horse had stumbled and he had drowned in the river, and that the second knight had been caught unawares from behind and thus could do little to protect himself. Sir Gareth met this with the same restraint he had shown all along until they reached a clearing in the midst of which sat a Black Knight, to whom the maiden rode over.

The Black Knight questioned the maiden as to her companion and she told him that Sir Gareth was no more than a kitchen worker who had been fed out of the charity of King Arthur and now accompanied her against her will. She then asked the Black Knight to rid her of Sir Gareth, adding that he should not be killed, but only wounded or frightened off. The Black Knight agreed and challenged Sir Gareth by saying that he was doing the maiden a disservice by riding with her, for she required the services of a man of noble birth and not a mere kitchenhand.

Sir Gareth replied that he had been born a gentleman of a better family than that of the Black Knight and would be pleased to prove it on the field of combat. For over an hour and a half they fought, until Sir Gareth threw the Black Knight from his horse and killed him. Seeing that his armour was better than his own, and presumably therefore better than that of Sir Kay, for Sir Gareth was wearing that knight's armour, he stripped the Black Knight, put on his armour, mounted the Black Knight's horse and rode off after the maiden. Shortly they were met by a Green Knight,[2] who hailed the maiden and asked her if she was in the company of his brother the Black Knight.

She replied that she was not and that a kitchenhand had killed his brother and taken his armour and horse. Upon hearing this, the Green Knight charged Sir Gareth, swearing that he would have revenge for the death of his brother, whom he named as Sir Percard. The two knights fought on until both were badly wounded. Finally Sir Gareth struck the Green Knight's helmet so hard that it brought him to his knees. Sir Gareth then took hold of the Green Knight's helmet and made ready to kill him, at which the Green Knight pleaded for mercy, saying that in return for his life he would serve Sir Gareth loyally and bring 30 more knights with him who would also serve him. Sir Gareth said that he would spare his life only if the maiden were to plead with him, but she refused, saying that she feared the Green Knight was in no danger from the kitchen worker. Three times the Green Knight beseeched her to beg for his life and finally she consented.

That night Sir Gareth and the maiden lodged with the Green Knight, who kept good his oath and brought forward 30 other knights, who pledged their allegiance to Sir Gareth. The following day Sir Gareth fought a Red Knight, Sir Perimones, the third of the three brothers, and likewise defeated him and spared his life at the request of the maiden. Sir Perimones also pledged his allegiance and brought 60 knights, who likewise swore an oath to Sir Gareth.

By this time the maiden was beginning to soften towards Sir Gareth, but she still taunted him about his humble origins. However, after he had defeated another knight, named in some sources as Sir Persant, who brought 100 knights who swore their allegiance to Sir Gareth, she softened completely and asked why Sir Gareth had endured her caustic tongue for so long. Sir Gareth replied that her words served only to strengthen his resolve. The maiden then begged forgiveness, which Sir Gareth gave unreservedly.

The following day Sir Gareth, the maiden and Sir Persant rode on to where Sir Ironside, the Red Knight of the Red Lands, was laying siege to a castle. Sir Persant stopped and would go no further, for he knew he would surely die if he met that knight in that place. However, here he deduced who the maiden was, and for the first time in the story it is revealed that she is Lynette, and that the lady of the castle is her sister Lyonesse. The siege had been going on for some two years and, though the Red Knight of the Red Lands could have gained entry at any time, he was hoping that Sir Lancelot or Sir Gawain or Sir Tristan would come and do combat with him.

Lynette, fully repentant now for the way she had treated Sir Gareth, turned to

Sir Persant and asked him if he would knight her companion. Sir Persant said he would gladly do so, whereupon Sir Gareth replied that there was no need for he had already been knighted by Sir Lancelot. He then added that he was Sir Gareth of Orkney, the brother of Sir Gawain, though neither he nor King Arthur, his uncle, knew this.

The dwarf who had been in the company of Sir Gareth and Lynette all the way from Arthur's court took news of the arrival of Sir Gareth to Lyonesse, who came out on to the battlements of her castle to see the knight of King Arthur's court who had come to champion her cause, sending the dwarf back out with provisions for the knight. Having eaten and rested, Lynette led Sir Gareth to the field of combat. There he saw 40 knights hanging from the trees around the perimeter, each of them having been killed by the Red Knight of the Red Lands.

Beside the castle stood a lone tree on which there hung a horn which Sir Gareth was to sound if he wished to do combat with the Red Knight of the Red Lands, though Lynette advised him to wait until noon, for in the morning his strength was that of ten men, but at noon he would only have the strength of a normal man. Sir Gareth would have nothing to do with such deceit, took up the horn and blew it hard.[3]

The Red Knight of the Red Lands appeared at the far end of the clearing and battle commenced, raging long and hard, neither knight ever really gaining the upper hand, until finally Sir Gareth overcame him and forced him to yield. Once again Sir Gareth spared the life of the vanquished knight. Lynette then treated the wounds of both knights before dispatching the Red Knight of the Red Lands to tell King Arthur of the deeds of the kitchen worker who had travelled with her to rescue her sister Lyonesse.

Sir Gareth, who had caught sight of Lyonesse on the battlements of her castle, Castle Perilous, and fallen in love with her, was presented to Lyonesse, who thanked him for saving her from the siege she had been under for more than two years. Sir Gareth told her of his love, but she, rather than saying no to his suit, put him off for a while and suggested that they should travel to the court of King Arthur, where his deeds could be recounted in full.

They were warmly greeted by all the knights at the court, save for Sir Kay whose wounds had yet to fully heal and who refused to believe in the might of a mere kitchenhand. Lyonesse, upon the advice of Sir Gareth, asked King Arthur to arrange a tournament at which the prize for the victor would be her hand and all her lands, unless of course that knight was already married, in which case the prize was to be a white peregrine falcon for the knight, a bird as prized then as it is today, and a crown of gold and precious stones for his wife.

A date was set for the tournament, which was to be held on the clearing in front of Castle Perilous, to which Lyonesse and Sir Gareth returned to make ready, Sir Gareth eliciting a promise from all those who knew of his true identity to keep it a secret. In preparation for the tournament Lyonesse gave Sir Gareth a ring that would ensure that, no matter how badly wounded he was, he would lose no blood, but made him promise to return it after the tournament, for the ring was the cause of her beauty.

Sir Gringamore, Lyonesse's brother, gave Sir Gareth a bay horse and the armour and sword that had once belonged to his father. Thus, on 15 August, the Feast of the Assumption,[4] the knights gathered on the field outside Castle Perilous and awaited the start of the tournament. At every joust Sir Gareth came off the best, but Sir Lancelot, even though asked to ride against the mysterious knight, would not. On one occasion two knights set about Sir Lancelot and Sir Gareth rode into their midst, but he never once cast at Sir Lancelot, who guessed the identity of the mystery knight. However, during a fight with his brother Sir Gawain, whose helmet Sir Gareth knocked off, Sir Gareth himself received a blow to his helmet which required repairing, so he briefly retired from the field of combat.

Sir Gareth dismounted, and the dwarf asked him to hand over the ring of Lyonesse for safekeeping. Sir Gareth did so, repaired his helmet, rested a while and then rejoined the combat, but forgot about the ring, which the dwarf had in his keeping. As he rode back on to the field, King Arthur noticed that the colour of the knight's armour had changed and now shone like gold. As no one could tell him who the mysterious knight was, King Arthur asked a herald to ride near to him and find out what he could. As the herald approached, he saw that the helmet was emblazoned with the words 'This helm belongs to Sir Gareth of Orkney'. Having read this, the herald proclaimed the name of the mysterious knight.

Angry that he had been discovered, Sir Gareth fought even more furiously, unseating both Sir Sagremor, the son of the King of Hungary, and Sir Gawain, who chided his brother for striking him. Hearing this, he cursed the dwarf for hiding the ring and rode swiftly off into the forest with his dwarf. There he commanded the dwarf to return the ring to Lyonesse, but would not go back to the field of combat. Instead he took to fighting all-comers in the forest, dispatching those who came and were defeated to do homage to King Arthur.

Some time later, while still living in the forest, Sir Gareth was doing combat with a knight when Lynette rode past and asked Sir Gareth why he fought his own brother Sir Gawain, for she had recognized the combatants. Sir Gawain immediately stopped fighting and embraced his brother. Lynette then attended to the wounds of both knights before riding off to bring King Arthur, who was just three kilometres (two miles) away, back to the scene of the fight. For eight days the company camped in the forest until both knights were healed. Lynette was then sent to bring Lyonesse to the camp.

When Lyonesse arrived, King Arthur asked Sir Gareth if he would take her as his wife. He replied that he would take no other. Arthur then asked Lyonesse, who replied that she would marry Sir Gareth or marry no one. The marriage of Sir

Gareth and Lyonesse was to be a three-pronged affair, for at the same service, held at Michaelmas,[5] Lynette married Sir Gawain and Sir Agravain married Laurel, a niece of Lyonesse. After the feast, which lasted for three days, a great tournament was organized, but, at the request of Lyonesse, only those knights who did not yet have a wife took part.

During Arthur's war against the Roman emperor Thereus, Gareth killed King Datis of Tuscany, but was himself to be killed by the fleeing though unarmed Lancelot, on the occasion when the latter was discovered in Queen Guinevere's bedchamber. However, some sources say that Sir Gareth was killed by Sir Lancelot when the latter rescued Guinevere moments before she was to be burned at the stake.

The story of Sir Gareth shows the extraordinary lengths to which a chivalrous knight was expected to go in order to uphold the honour of the fair sex. No matter how humble that knight's origins might appear, he had clear objectives: to do his king's bidding, to fight honourably and nobly, and to act in a manner that none could find fault with. Sir Gareth did all this and much more, for even though he was of noble birth, he gladly humbled himself to prove his worth and would let no one come between him and his goal.

Sir Gawain

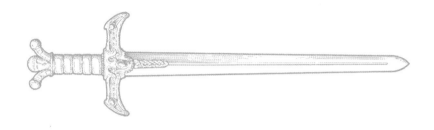

ONE OF THE MOST PROMINENT of Arthur's knights, Gawain was the oldest
son of Lot and Morgause, though in Welsh tradition there appears to be
a degree of confusion over his parentage. Sometimes Gwyar is given as his
father, sometimes as his mother. In French romances his name is variously given as
Gauvain, Gauwain, Gayain, and so on; in Latin he is Walganus (Geoffrey of
Monmouth calls him Walgainus); in Dutch Walewein and in Irish Balbhuaidh.
Welsh tradition calls him Gwalchmai fab Gwyar ('fab Gwyar' meaning 'son of
Gwyar') – 'hawk of May' or 'hawk of the plain' – but it has been argued, some
think successfully, that Gwalchmai and Gawain were originally different characters,
the Welsh simply identifying their Gwalchmai with the Continental Gawain. Others
have, with almost equal success, argued that the two have always been identical. In
origin, if Gwalchmai and Gawain were always the same character, he appears to be
the *Mabinogion* character Gwrvan Gwallt-avwy, a name that seems to have been
derived from the Welsh *gwallt-avwyn* ('hair like rain') or *gwallt-advwyn* ('fair hair'). He
is also possibly to be identified with the hero of a Scottish tale, *Uallabh*.[1]

The story of Gawain is variously given, but aside from minor differences is
basically as follows.

He was the son of King Lot of Lothian. Lot was, in his early days, a page to
Arthur's sister Morgause, on whom he fathered Gawain. The Latin *De Ortu
Waluuanii* ('The Rise of Gawain') makes his mother Anna rather than Morgause.
Having been baptized, he was set adrift in a cask. He was eventually rescued by
fishermen, made his way to Rome and was knighted by Pope Sulpicius.[2] Arriving
at Arthur's court, he became one of that king's most prominent knights, depicted
in early romance as a great champion. However, he is less likeable in later works
that were influenced by the writing of Sir Thomas Malory, who seems to have taken

a particular dislike to him. French romances, on the whole, portray Gawain as promiscuous in the extreme.

Various tales give Gawain different wives, including Amurfine; Ragnell, the loathsome hag to whom he was pledged in marriage by Arthur in return for answering a riddle none of his court had been able to, though she is sometimes referred to as the daughter of Sir Gilbert and sister of Brandiles and two unnamed brothers; the daughter of the king of the unidentified realm of Sorcha, named in some sources as Ragnell; and the daughter of the Carl of Carlisle, who gave him her hand in marriage in return for Gawain's breaking the enchantment he was held under. Italian romance made him the lover of Pulzella Gaia ('Cheerful Damsel'), the daughter of Morgan Le Fay by Hemison,[3] while he was the husband or lover of Ysabele in the thirteenth century Middle Dutch *Walewein*. His sons are named as Florence and Lovel by Amurfine, and Guinglain by Ragnell.

Sir Gawain features in many of the other Arthurian legends, though he does not really develop until relatively late in the cycle. Usually he is depicted as a staunch supporter of King Arthur, and the loyal friend of many at court, even though some of those with whom he is on friendly terms are not well thought of in other quarters. This is particularly true when it comes to the likes of his brothers, for Sir Gawain comes from the one family that supplied more knights, or generations of knights, to the Round Table than any other family, including that of King Arthur (see page 39).

Following the death of many of his family and friends at the hands of Lancelot when they attempted to capture him *in flagrante delicto* with Guinevere, and Lancelot's departure from the court, Gawain became violently opposed to Lancelot and would have done anything in his power to dispose of him. Gawain accompanied Arthur on his Continental expedition against the Roman Empire and latterly against Sir Lancelot. Landing back in Britain, he was killed with a club at the second battle against Sir Mordred at Winchester, though according to Breton tradition he survived the last battle of Camlann and actually succeeded Arthur, who abdicated in his favour. His death at Winchester did not mark his last appearance, for his ghost was reputed to have advised Arthur in the run-up to the battle of Camlann.

The owner of a horse named Gringalet, Gawain had the strange power of becoming stronger towards noon, while his strength diminished again during the afternoon. This same trait has also been attributed to Escanor, one of Gawain's enemies. This peculiar gift appears to be Welsh in origin, as this is the special skill attributed to Gwalchmai, who was one of the party picked to help Culhwch in his quest to locate Olwen. He may therefore have a solar origin, possibly being a memory of some ancient sun god. Connection has also been made between Gawain and Cú Chulainn, the archetypal Irish warrior, who, like Gawain, owned an enchanted belt that rendered the wearer invulnerable.

William of Malmesbury reports that his grave was discovered during the reign of King William II (1087–1100) at Ros, though this location cannot be determined with any certainty. His skull was supposed to have been held in Dover Castle, Kent.

Gawain participated in a beheading contest with a giant, the story appearing in the tales of *Sir Gawain and the Green Knight* (*c*.1346), *Sir Gawain and the Carl of Carlisle* (*c*.1400) and *The Turk and Gawain* (*c*.1500). This story, which has similarities with the Irish story of Cú Chulainn, possibly represents a memory of some earlier pagan hero who was the prototype of Gawain. Some have maintained that Gawain is identical with Cú Chulainn, this association being drawn not just from the similarity of the stories but also from the fact that the tale seems to come from the north of England. In ancient times a tribe known as the Setantii lived in this region and the original name of Cú Chulainn was Setanta. It is not very hard to see how this link was arrived at. The famous yet anonymous *Sir Gawain and the Green Knight* gives possibly the best known account of this episode.

During the New Year's festivities at Camelot, as was his custom, King Arthur was refusing to eat until some adventure had befallen the assembled company. Just then a huge knight appeared, clad all in green and riding a green horse. This Green Knight demanded to see Arthur, who inquired what the knight wanted. The mysterious knight proposed that he would allow any of Arthur's knights to strike off his head provided he be allowed to retaliate in the same manner the following year. As all the knights were in awe of the strange knight's appearance, they hesitated, which made the Green Knight taunt them for their cowardice. King Arthur leapt to his feet in anger to take up the challenge and would have done so had not Sir Gawain restrained him and asked for permission to undertake the challenge himself. Arthur agreed and Gawain beheaded the Green Knight, who, much to the astonishment of the onlookers, calmly picked up his severed head and reminded Sir Gawain to meet him at the Green Chapel in a year's time. The Green Knight galloped away with his head tucked neatly under his arm.

A year later Gawain was *en route* for the rematch when he found himself in the midst of a vast forest. Fearing for his safety he knelt and prayed. Resuming his journey he soon came to a mysterious castle where he was warmly greeted and entertained by the lord, who told him that, as the Green Chapel was but a short distance away, Gawain might lodge there until it was time for him to meet the Green Knight. Gawain and his host agreed that, during his stay, they would exchange with each other what they had obtained during the day.

On the first day, while his host was out hunting, Gawain received a kiss from his host's wife, which was duly passed on when the lord gave him the results of his day's hunting. Likewise, Gawain passed on the two kisses he received from his hostess the following evening. However, on the third day Gawain received three kisses and some green lace, which his hostess told him would protect him. That evening only the kisses were passed on.

The following day Sir Gawain departed and rode the short distance to the Green Chapel where he duly met the Green Knight. Gawain knelt to receive the blow. Three times the Green Knight aimed his sword at Sir Gawain's neck. Twice he failed to make contact, and the third time only nicked him. Sir Gawain arose, upon which the Green Knight revealed himself to be none other than his host of the last three days, Bertilak de Hautdesert, and said that he would not have cut Gawain at all had he been told of the lace.

Gawain's remorse at this act is marked by four beautiful lines, which are to be found close to the end of the poem, after he has returned to Camelot and told them all that has passed.

He groaned at his disgrace,
Unfolding his ill-fame,
And blood suffused his face,
When he showed his mark of shame.

Another story concerning Gawain comes from the vicinity of Carlisle during the days when Arthur was said to have held his court there; it is related in a traditional border ballad. Outside the city walls Arthur was overpowered by a local knight who spared his life on the condition that within a year he would return with the answer to the question 'What is it that women most desire?' No one at court could supply the answer, so Arthur was honour-bound to return to the knight when the year had elapsed and forfeit his life. On his way to the meeting, Arthur was approached by a hideous woman who told him that she would give him the answer, provided the king found a husband for her. Arthur agreed and the hag told him that the one thing women desire most is to have their own way. The answer was related to the knight and, as it proved correct, Arthur's life was spared. Returning to his court he appointed Sir Gawain to be the ugly woman's husband, thus fulfilling his promise.

Though hideous beyond comprehension, Gawain always treated her with knightly courtesy, and in return the woman offered Gawain a reward. She would become beautiful either by day or by night, the choice was his. Remembering the answer she had given Arthur, Gawain told her that she might have her own way and choose for herself. His chivalrous answer broke the enchantment under which she had been held, and she immediately became beautiful by both day and night. Some sources name this woman as Ragnell, the daughter of the King of Sorcha, but this maiden is usually identified as the daughter of Sir Gilbert.

Commentators seeking the origins of the Arthurian characters have suggested that Gawain was originally Arthur's son, as the story of Gawain's birth and his subsequently being set adrift, mirrors that of Mordred. This version of events suggests that Gawain was the incestuous son of Arthur and his sister who was Morgan Le Fay in the original story. The shift from Morgan Le Fay to Morgause does not take much imagination. It has also been suggested that Gawain was originally one of the Grail questers but was later replaced by Galahad due to the former's pagan origins and continuing associations. Similarly, Sir Perceval has been mooted as the replacement character.

Later literature has amended the character of Sir Gawain quite considerably. He was always portrayed as chivalrous, as his position as a Knight of the Round Table would demand, but he became progressively more churlish. Early writers, such as Geoffrey of Monmouth and Robert Wace, describe him as the bravest of Arthur's knights. Though his loyalty to King Arthur was never called into question, he appears to have developed into a foil for Sir Kay, whom he almost seems to replace in terms of impertinence in the later renditions of the Arthurian legends, as well as many of the other Knights of the Round Table – Lancelot, Yvain and the like. Chrétien de Troyes starts the degeneration by saying that he is promiscuous but still a heroic figure, noted for his chivalry. However, by the time *Perceval* was published after Chrétien de Troyes's death in 1183, it was clear that Gawain resented the other knights whom he felt were being exalted in his place. Later still, his character deteriorated into something of a joke. In the anonymous *Queste del Sainte Graal* and *Tristan*, Gawain is portrayed as callous, selfish and a murderer, thus epitomizing the very worst aspects of knighthood. It is interesting to note, however, that all these developments in the character of Gawain are French, for in Britain, the Low Countries and Germany, Gawain remained the pre-eminent Arthurian hero, a fact that is perhaps best portrayed in the famous *Sir Gawain and the Green Knight*, for in that poem, having just nicked him, the Green Knight freely admits that Sir Gawain is 'the most perfect paladin ever to pace the earth'. It remains a mystery why the French should have taken such a dislike to Sir Gawain. No doubt if the author of *Sir Gawain and the Green Knight* had been French, Sir Gawain would have dearly relished the idea of being openly seduced by the wife of the Green Knight.

Sir Kay

THE VERY FIRST REFERENCES TO SIR KAY appear in the early Welsh legends, where he was known as Cai, Cei or Kai. He appears in the *Mabinogion* story of *Culhwch and Olwen*, in which he was chosen to be among the party formed to help Culhwch in his quest to locate and marry Olwen. All the members of the party were chosen for their special skills, those of Cei being that he could remain nine days and nine nights without either breathing or sleeping, could change his height at will and had a body temperature so high that he never got wet, while in cold weather fires could be kindled from him. Cei clearly had a cunning nature, for on one occasion during the quest to locate Olwen, Cei and his companions rested with a giant named Gwrnach, one of Yspaddaden's enemies, and by pretending to be a sword-polisher, Cei tricked the giant out of his sword.

Cei was later to resurface as Sir Kay, the devious son of Ector and foster brother of Arthur. Though appearing in the earlier romances as a model of chivalry, later stories made him a troublesome and somewhat childish character who believed that his relationship to Arthur gave him the right to behave in any way he chose. Kay owned a horse known as Gwinam Goddwf Hir, a name that has obviously spilled over from his early Welsh name Cei, and married Andrivete, the daughter of King Cador of Northumberland, an act that some say was the only truly good thing he did throughout his career, for Andrivete had had the kingdom of Northumberland usurped from her by her uncle Ayglin, who wanted her to marry a man of his choosing. Andrivete escaped and married Kay, who persuaded his foster brother Arthur to march against Ayglin, but that proved unnecessary, as Ayglin was forced to surrender by the people of Northumberland, who reinstated Andrivete. Kay and Andrivete are credited with a daughter named Kelemon, and two sons called Garanwyn and Gronois. Kay's brief genealogy is shown right.

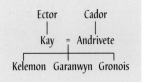

Originally Kay claimed that it was he and not Arthur who had withdrawn the Sword in the Stone, but Ector compelled him to tell the truth. The story is as follows.

After the death of Uther, as there was no heir to the throne, Britain fell into disarray as numerous knights attempted to seize the crown for themselves. To determine who had the right to rule, Merlin and the then Archbishop of Canterbury decided that a tournament would be held. The date for the contest was to be the following Christmas Day, though some sources say that the tournament came about only as an afterthought, and that the assembly in London was to decide, by democratic methods, who should become king. All the knights of the realm descended on London, including Ector, his son Kay, who was to be knighted, and his foster son Arthur who had been placed in his care some 15 years earlier by Merlin.

In a churchyard near to where the tournament was to be held there stood a stone in which was embedded a sword emblazoned with the words: 'Whosoever shall draw this sword from the stone is the true born King of all England.' Many knights had tried, but all had failed. The alternative to this story says that on Christmas Day all the assembled knights gathered at an unnamed church to celebrate Mass, but before they could enter the church the sword in the stone appeared among them. Sir Ector, Kay and Arthur were not present on this occasion, as they were still on their way to London. Even though all the knights there wanted to try to remove the sword immediately, the Archbishop of Canterbury insisted that they celebrate Mass first, for there would be plenty of time afterwards to see who became king.

After Mass had been duly celebrated, all the knights gathered around the mystical sword, and, each waiting impatiently in line, they tried to remove the sword. None managed it. Merlin and the Archbishop of Canterbury deliberated on what to do next and then announced that a great tournament would be held, the victor of which would be crowned king until such time as someone managed to remove the sword from the stone. The tournament, it was agreed, was to be held on New Year's Day.

On the morning of the tournament Ector, Kay and Arthur left their dwellings for the tournament field, but upon arriving Kay found that Arthur, who was acting as his squire, had forgotten to bring his sword. Arthur immediately left to fetch it, but when he returned to their lodgings he found the door barred as the innkeeper and all his family had left to watch the tournament. Distressed that he should have failed his brother, Arthur trudged back to the tournament to break the news to Kay. *En route* he passed the sword in the stone and, chancing his arm, removed it with ease. He then returned to Kay and gave him the sword, not realizing the significance of what he had done.

Kay, on the other hand, immediately recognized the sword and ran to his father, shouting that he had drawn the sword, and so should be proclaimed king. Ector was none too sure about this, even though he knew what ownership of the sword conferred, as Kay had earlier tried and failed. Ector therefore took Kay and Arthur back to the stone and there made Kay place his hand on a Bible and tell him how he had come by the sword. Kay could do nothing else but tell the truth.

Ector then turned to Arthur and had him replace the sword and pull it out again, which he did with consummate ease. As soon as Ector and Kay witnessed this, they sank to their knees in respect, a position which both amused and embarrassed Arthur, who still did not realize exactly what he had done. Ector then explained to Arthur the significance of the sword and for the first time revealed that, in fact, Uther Pendragon and not he himself was Arthur's father, Arthur having been placed in his care by Merlin.

News that the sword had been pulled from the stone quickly spread, and soon Arthur, Ector and Kay were in the midst of a huge throng of people, both knights and the general populace, who had gathered to see if the news was indeed true. When Arthur once again removed the sword, the Archbishop of Canterbury proclaimed Arthur to be king, and many fell to their knees to do him homage and to pledge their allegiance. However, 11 mighty barons refused to accept the 15-year old Arthur as their king and so his reign started in turmoil.

Arthur made Kay his seneschal (steward),[1] and promised that while he remained king Kay would hold that position, the highest he could bestow. It is this promise that led to the impertinence of Sir Kay, who would cruelly deride everyone, including Arthur and Guinevere, and get away with it every time, even though he would often be challenged to do combat over some flippant remark he had made. On one such occasion, the youthful Perceval had just arrived at the court and asked to be admitted, but Kay jeered at him, saying that such a shabbily dressed person could never be allowed in, and that if he truly desired to gain entry, he would first have to meet a knight in combat. By chance, a ruffian knight, one of the many Red Knights of the Arthurian cycle, had that very day challenged the whole of the court of King Arthur by throwing a goblet of wine into the face of Guinevere. Perhaps, so Kay sneered, Perceval would care to do them all the service of dispatching the rogue. Perceval cheerily turned about, killed the knight and was admitted to the court when he arrived back there wearing the defeated knight's armour, even though Kay clearly thought that he would have seen the last of the troublesome youth. This story is told in more detail in the profile for Sir Perceval (see pages 143–6).

Many different stories are told about Kay, some obscure and some well known. The thirteenth-century French prose romance *Perlesvaus*, which deals mainly with the quest for the Holy Grail, recounts how he killed Loholt, Arthur's son, and joined Brian des Illes in a rebellion against the king. This story further adds that Arthur apparently broke his promise to Kay and Ector that Kay would remain his seneschal for as long as he was king, for in *Perlesvaus* Brian des Illes is made Arthur's seneschal after he swears allegiance to the king, Kay possibly being fired as punishment for his treachery. The accounts of Kay's death vary. Throughout Welsh literature and tradition he was said to have been killed by Gwyddawg, who was in turn killed by Arthur. He was also said to have been killed during Arthur's campaign against the Roman Empire, or in the war against Mordred. One source numbers him among the knights killed by the escaping yet unarmed Lancelot when the latter had been caught in compromising circumstances in Guinevere's bedchamber.

Though the character of Sir Kay remains little altered throughout the Arthurian cycle, his behaviour in early texts is probably at worst childish, whereas in later texts he is openly defiant. Perhaps Sir Kay still held on to the belief that he and not Arthur should have been king, and was never going to let Arthur, or anyone else come to that, forget that Arthur might never have been proclaimed king if it had not been for him.

Having been raised with the young Arthur, and then being made Arthur's steward even before the actual start of Arthur's reign, Kay clearly felt at liberty to do as he pleased, secure in the knowledge of the pledge Arthur had made to his father and with little fear, therefore, that he would be punished by Arthur as he so often deserved. *Perlesvaus* begs to differ. On more than one occasion Sir Kay is bested by a more honourable and likeable knight, but he never seems to learn his lesson. For all this, though, Sir Kay remained loyal to his foster brother, which has to redeem his character, if only by a small amount.

Sir Lancelot

THE MOST FAMOUS OF ALL Arthur's knights, the king's champion, friend and confidant, Lancelot is truly a knight in shining armour and a most complex character. Different commentators are still undecided on his origin. Was he Celtic or merely the invention of the Continentals? His name is generally regarded as a double diminutive of the German word *Land*, though it has been argued, some feel successfully, that Llwch Lleminawc, a character who accompanies Arthur to the Otherworld in the *Preiddeu Annwfn* ('Spoils of Annwfn'),[1] is his original. By the same token, this journey has been identified with the expedition Arthur makes to Ireland in the *Mabinogion* story of *Culhwch and Olwen* and if this is indeed the case, Lancelot appears to number among the accompanying party as Llenlleawc, though in this instance an Irishman. These identifications have been called into doubt by the appearance of the names Lanslod and Lawnslot, which seem to have been used to translate Lancelot from other languages into Welsh. This is certainly possible, and may be a retranslation of Lancelot back into Welsh when those writers who came across the name Lancelot failed to recognize its origins in Llwch Lleminawc or Llenlleawc.

Celtic origins certainly figure in the version of Lancelot's story told by Ulrich von Zarzikhoven, the Swiss or German author (*fl*. 1200) of *Lanzelet*, which differs quite markedly from the accounts of the life of Lancelot as told by Chrétien de Troyes and other romancers. Here, Lancelot is the son of King Pant of Gennewis and Clarine. As his father had been killed during an uprising, Lancelot was taken away by a fairy and raised in the Otherworldly realm of Maidenland,[2] but she would not tell him his name until he had fought Iweret of Beforet, who was, according to both Ulrich von Zarzikhoven and Wolfram von Eschenbach, the father of Iblis. He was trained as a knight and in the use of all manner of weapons

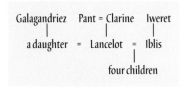

by Johfrit de Liez, an inhabitant of Maidenland, and married the daughter of Galagandriez. The fairy had a son, Mabuz, whose lands were being invaded by Iweret, whom Lancelot fought and killed, thus learning his name. He married Iblis, Iweret's daughter, and had four children by her, and eventually won back the kingdom of his father, Pant. The appearance of Mabuz, who is thought to have originated in the Celtic god Mabon, certainly indicates that Lancelot had a Celtic origin. Parts of this story tally with the more familiar story of Lancelot as related in French and German sources, as well as by Sir Thomas Malory. Ulrich von Zarzikhoven determines Lancelot's family tree as shown here:

The more usual version of Lancelot's story is, in essence, as follows.

The son of King Ban and Elaine, he was left on the shores of a lake by his mother after Ban had died. He was found by the Lady of the Lake (not necessarily the same Lady of the Lake who was the custodian of Excalibur), who raised him, and through this he became known as Lancelot of the Lake. Having grown to manhood, he was taken to Arthur's court by his foster mother, who asked that Arthur himself should knight him. This Arthur did, so Lancelot became a Knight of the Round Table, and before long was Arthur's most trusted companion. However, just as Merlin had foretold, he quickly fell in love with Guinevere, who presented him with a sword at his investiture as he had forgotten to bring his own. The queen reciprocated his feelings, and so began the famous, and sometimes stormy, love affair between them.

During his many adventures, Lancelot visited Castle Carbonek and there rescued the maiden Elaine from a bath of boiling water, though this rescue is also said to have taken place in a brazen tower some distance away from the castle. Other reports further describe the tower as the fairest Lancelot had ever seen. Lancelot was entertained by King Pelles, Elaine's father. The king and Brisen, Elaine's handmaiden (or, alternatively, an enchantress), conspired to have Lancelot sleep with Elaine, for it had been prophesied that he should father the purest knight on her, though just who made this prophecy is never revealed. At a feast in Lancelot's honour, during which, according to some sources, Brisen administered a love potion, Lancelot became enchanted into thinking that Elaine was Guinevere and subsequently lay with her. As a result Galahad was conceived. Later the two slept together again (once more with the help of Brisen's magic), this time at Camelot, but they were discovered by the furious Guinevere, who banished her lover from the court. He went mad, running wild in the forests, sometimes tended by hermits and village folk. Only after many years was he restored to sanity by the Grail, the holy vessel for which he subsequently searched.

His participation in the quest for the Holy Grail depicts a very vivid image of the trials and tribulations of Sir Lancelot, for he had tried with all his might to remain a pure knight but circumstances dictated otherwise. The legends do not say whether or not Lancelot embarked on the quest from Camelot, but it seems likely that he was not at the court when the quest started as he had been banished by Guinevere, though given the confused chronology of the Arthurian cycle this cannot be known for certain.

After many months of fruitless and lonely searching Sir Lancelot came to a stone cross near a derelict chapel. Tying his horse to the cross and hanging his shield on a nearby branch, Lancelot walked towards the chapel. Through the broken door he saw an altar covered with a silk cloth on which stood a six-branched candlestick from which a pure light emanated, a light that disabled Sir Lancelot so much that he had only just enough energy to crawl back to the cross. He took his shield from the tree, and lay down on it to sleep.

As he lay there, half asleep and half awake, he saw two white palfreys (saddle horses) come by, drawing a litter on which was a sick knight. As the litter drew alongside Sir Lancelot, who found himself unable to move, the wounded knight beseeched God to save him from death from his injuries. Instantly the candlestick on the altar appeared at the foot of the cross, along with a silver table on which stood the Holy Grail. Immediately the sick knight rose from the litter, completely cured of all his ailments. The Grail, table and candlestick then returned to the chapel and Sir Lancelot, who had watched these events, fell into a heavy sleep.

When Sir Lancelot awoke he found that the knight he had seen being so miraculously cured had taken his sword, his helmet and his horse. Knowing that his earthly sins had prevented him from receiving the Communion of the Grail, Lancelot left the chapel on foot, lamenting the very day he had been born.

Lancelot walked for many days through a thick forest, dwelling with the numerous hermits he came across, until he met with and successfully defeated the knight who had stolen his sword, helmet and horse, and so recovered these items. That night he again lodged with a hermit in the forest. This man told him that Sir Galahad was his son and that he was the one who had come to Arthur's court and sat in the Siege Perilous, which was reserved for the best knight in all the world.

The following morning, his spirits somewhat lifted by the news that Sir Galahad was his son – though some sources insist that he already knew this – Sir Lancelot rode until he came to a castle outside which at least 500 knights were doing combat, those nearest the castle dressed all in black, astride black horses, and those attacking them in white armour on white horses. Lancelot watched until he determined that the Black Knights were faring the worst and then joined the combat on their side, fighting on until he was so exhausted that his arms could not lift his sword. Then the white knights carried him off into the forest so that he might rest and there left him alone.

Having regained his strength, Lancelot rode away from the castle through the forest until he came to a small chapel, wherein he found a nun who asked him his name and what his purpose was. Sir Lancelot told her all that had befallen him.

She told him that the Black Knights he had ridden to help were a representation of earthly sin, while the White Knights were a representation of righteousness. When he learned this, Lancelot felt even more ashamed of his conduct, for by fighting for the Black Knights he had been on the side of earthly sin and vanity and had only compounded his own sins.

Some time later Sir Lancelot found himself beside a vast expanse of water and he lay down to sleep. In that sleep a voice told him to rise up and enter the first ship he should come across. Lancelot immediately started down the shore and soon came to a ship that had neither oars nor sail but that none the less set off as soon as he had stepped on board. Lancelot was filled with a sense of peace and joy, and quickly fell asleep. When he awoke, he discovered a bed in the middle of the ship upon which lay the body of Perceval's sister, Dindrane, and in her hand was a letter explaining how she had died, though it does not appear that the Sword of the Strange Hangings was on board at this particular time, that sword possibly still being in the ownership of Sir Galahad (see profile, pages 87–91).

For months the ship sailed on, until one day it came close to a strange shore. A knight appeared, coming aboard the moment the ship touched the beach, and they instantly set out to sea again. This knight was Sir Galahad and this was the first meeting between the two since they had started on their quest. For six months the little ship continued to travel while father and son recounted all their strange adventures. At the end of that time, the ship came to the edge of a forest where Lancelot and Galahad saw a knight astride a white horse holding the reins of another. As the ship came in to land and Lancelot and Galahad disembarked, the knight spoke to Galahad, telling him to rejoin the quest for the Holy Grail.

Galahad and Lancelot made their farewells, each knowing that they would not see the other again in their time on earth. After watching his son disappear into the forest, Sir Lancelot once more placed his trust in the small ship, which, after a month at sea, beached at midnight beside a fine castle. A door opened out towards the sea and a voice bade Lancelot enter. Arming himself for the adventure he knew lay ahead, Lancelot approached the gate, where, seeing two lions standing guard, he drew his sword. As he did so it was struck from his hand by some unseen force and a voice chided him for being of little faith, for he apparently put more trust in his weapons than he did in his maker.

Without further challenge, Lancelot entered the castle, but once inside he could find no door that would open for him. Behind one door he heard sweet and reverent singing and knew full well that the Grail was there. Dropping to his knees, Sir Lancelot prayed to God that he should be shown at least some part of the Grail. Looking up, he saw the door swinging slowly open. A green light shone from the room, a light that was the cleanest and the purest Lancelot had ever seen. Within the light was a silver table on which stood the Holy Grail, covered in red samite, and all the ornaments of an altar, along with a priest who seemed to celebrate Mass.

Lancelot could no longer bear to remain outside the room, so he strode into the chamber and reached out to touch the holy vessel. As he stretched out his arm, a scorching wind threw him to the ground. Unable to move, he felt hands all around him that carried him out of the room to deposit him in the passage. The following morning the people of the castle found Lancelot's inert body and carried him to a bedchamber, where he lay without stirring. On the twenty-fifth day, Lancelot awoke and, realizing that he had achieved as much of the Grail as he was to be allowed, gave thanks to God and made his way back to Camelot. There he was greeted warmly, but he found that more than half of the Knights of the Round Table had been killed during the quest.

Having returned to Arthur's court, Lancelot once again took up his affair with Guinevere, but Arthur still refused to believe that the rumours about Lancelot and his wife were true. Lancelot championed the queen's cause when she was abducted by Meleagaunce, the son of King Bagdemagus. *En route* for the castle to which Meleagaunce had taken Guinevere, Lancelot was ambushed by a party of archers who had been placed to guard the road by Meleagaunce and had his horse shot from under him. Lancelot was not to be stopped that easily and continued on foot until he came to a peasant leading a horse and cart. Though reluctant to ride in such a lowly vehicle, Lancelot was so weary that he asked to be conveyed to the castle of Meleagaunce. Once there, Lancelot crossed a 'sword bridge' to reach the castle in which Meleagaunce had taken refuge with his hostage, whom he had planned to rape, though he had been stopped by his father. Lancelot and Meleagaunce fought in single combat, but Bagdemagus pleaded with Guinevere to save his son, so the fight was stopped on the condition it be taken up in one year's time. Some sources, however, make Lancelot fare much worse and become the prisoner of Meleagaunce, who returned Guinevere to Arthur but left Lancelot to die in his dungeon, which he would have done had he not been fed by one of Meleagaunce's maids who also helped Lancelot to escape and exact his revenge. Later Meleagaunce accused Guinevere of committing adultery with Kay, and once again Lancelot championed her cause. Again Bagdemagus had to plead for his son's life, which was on this occasion spared, but Lancelot finally killed Meleagaunce in combat at Arthur's court.

Once more Lancelot came to the rescue of Guinevere after she had been accused of murdering Sir Petroc by Sir Mador, this story being told in the profile of Sir Bors (see pages 81–5). Reinstated at the Round Table again, Lancelot began his affair with Guinevere afresh. She, however, was not the only lady to love Lancelot, for he was also loved by Elaine, the daughter of Bernard of Astolat,[3] who pledged her love for him while he was *en route* for a tournament, even though she did not know his name and he would not reveal it.

Desiring to attend the tournament in disguise, Sir Lancelot borrowed the shield of Elaine's brother, Sir Tirre, and wore Elaine's favour in the form of a red sleeve tied to his helmet. Thus disguised and in the company of Elaine's younger brother, Sir Lavaine, though some sources make Lavaine the sister of Elaine, Lancelot rode forth to the tournament at Camelot. There King Arthur recognized Sir Lancelot but kept the secret, even though at one stage Sir Gawain almost guessed that the mysterious knight who was fighting so marvellously was none other than Lancelot himself. Lancelot fought long and hard until he was wounded when the head of Sir Bors's lance broke off in his side. When Sir Lavaine saw this, he rode among the mêlée and fought off those knights who were around the stricken Sir Lancelot. Seeing that he was wounded, King Arthur had his heralds announce that the tournament had been won by the mystery knight who had unseated more knights than anyone else. Once Sir Lancelot had been awarded the prize, he and Sir Lavaine rode off into the forest to attend to Lancelot's wounds.

A short distance away lived a hermit whom Lancelot knew could heal his wounds, so he had Sir Lavaine take him straight there. The hermit dressed the wounds, and tended the knight, who would take much healing. Back at Camelot there was considerable discussion about who the mysterious knight might have been, but still King Arthur kept his silence, for in truth even he was not totally sure. The area around the tournament was searched, but no sign of the knight could be found, so Gawain set out and soon came to Astolat, where he lodged with Sir Bernard. There he told his host of the tournament and of the demise of a knight who wore the red sleeve of a maiden as his token.

Elaine overheard the conversation and told Sir Gawain that she had loved the knight whose name she did not know. She took Gawain to where she had hidden Lancelot's shield in the hope that Gawain could tell her who he was. When Sir Gawain saw the shield, he sobbed and told Elaine that the shield belonged to Sir Lancelot, the best knight in the kingdom, and that his death, for surely his wounds would have killed him, would be lamented for many years to come. Elaine refused to believe that Lancelot was dead and set out to search for him herself.

Some time later, Elaine came across her brother Lavaine, who took her to where Lancelot lay in the care of the hermit, his life still in danger. At about the same time, Gawain had returned to Arthur's court and told the king that the mystery knight was none other than Sir Lancelot. News of this reached Guinevere who was furious that Lancelot should carry the token of another maiden. She sent for Sir Bors, who tried to reason with her, but Guinevere would have none of it, calling Sir Lancelot a traitor. Lancelot, aware that his identity would be known by now, sent for Lavaine and had him fetch Sir Bors to the hermitage. Bors stayed there until Lancelot was fully healed, before returning to Camelot to tell Arthur of Sir Lancelot's recovery, but also to tell Guinevere that Lancelot had worn the colours of another lady only to hide his identity.

Lancelot returned to Astolat, where the fair Elaine pleaded with him to make her his wife. Lancelot refused as kindly as he could and returned to Camelot, where he was openly greeted by Arthur and all the Knights of the Round Table, save Sir Mordred and Sir Agravain. Guinevere would have nothing to do with him and Lancelot became a sorry figure. Elaine, knowing that her love would never be requited, refused to eat or drink and within a few short weeks she died. Her last act was to have her father write a letter explaining how and why she had died. He placed this letter in her hand before setting her body on a barge that was to be floated down the Thames to Westminster, where Arthur and Guinevere were holding court.[4]

There the barge was pulled in and both Arthur and Guinevere came to pay their respects to the young maiden whose body had appeared in such curious circumstances. Finding the letter, Arthur called together the Knights of the Round Table and read its contents aloud. The letter said that Lancelot was the only knight Elaine could ever have loved, and as he did not love her then she must die, for to live would be too painful. Arthur charged Lancelot with ensuring that Elaine received a proper and befitting burial. Guinevere, at last aware of the truth, forgave Lancelot, which allowed their affair to begin once more.

Shortly afterwards, Lancelot's adultery with Guinevere was yet again brought to Arthur's attention, and yet again he refused to believe it unless conclusive evidence could be brought before him. Finally Lancelot and Guinevere were trapped together in the queen's bedchamber by Sir Mordred, Sir Agravain and 12 other knights. Lancelot, though unarmed, managed to fight his way to freedom, killing all but Sir Mordred, who took news of the queen's infidelity to Arthur. The king had no option other than to sentence Guinevere to be burned at the stake for treason. News of Guinevere's sentence reached Lancelot, who rushed back to Arthur's court and rescued the hapless queen moments before the fire was lit, though in so doing he killed many of the remaining Knights of the Round Table. He then took her to his castle, Joyous Gard, which is usually said to have been located in France but has been identified by some with Bamburgh Castle in Northumberland.

Even now, wary of Merlin's prophecies, Arthur wanted nothing more than to make peace with his old friend, but he mistakenly took the advice of his nephew Mordred, who had designs on the throne, and went to war against Lancelot. Mordred was left as his regent. Arthur laid siege to Lancelot's castle for 15 weeks, but never once were the walls breached. Finally, with the intervention of the Pope, Lancelot successfully championed Guinevere in single combat and thus earned her pardon. The queen returned to Arthur, who immediately sent her home to England, while his battle against Lancelot continued.

In Arthur's absence, Mordred had usurped the throne and, upon the return of Guinevere, he set about spreading false news of Arthur's death so that he might legally be proclaimed king. He additionally stated that he was to marry Guinevere, who immediately went to London, where she barricaded herself in the Tower of

London with sufficient provisions for a lengthy siege.[5] News of these events reached Arthur, who instantly stopped his fight with Lancelot and returned to deal with the situation at home. News of Sir Mordred's treachery, however, did not reach Lancelot until some time later. At once he set off for England, but arrived one month after the final battle of Camlann, and was thus too late to help his old friend. He travelled to Amesbury, where Guinevere had taken the veil, and after talking with her and realizing that she was lost to him, he went to Glastonbury, where he became a monk. He returned to Amesbury some years later, following a dream that told him to ride there as fast as he could. He arrived too late, for Guinevere had died not half an hour before. Grief-stricken, Lancelot carried her body to Glastonbury, where, according to later accounts that were written after Glastonbury had become equated with Avalon, he buried her body next to that of Arthur. In his distress, Lancelot could neither eat nor sleep, and within a matter of a few short weeks he too had died.

Throughout the legends that surround Sir Lancelot, it is clear that even though his love for the queen was illicit and ill-founded, there was no malice in any of his actions, and apart from the sin of loving the wife of another, he remains a shining example of the medieval ideal of a chivalrous knight who would gladly lay down his life for king, for country and for Christendom. Though Lancelot puts in his first appearance in *Le chevalier de la charette*, which was composed by Chrétien de Troyes around 1170, he quickly found his way into the hearts of a great many medieval authors. It is interesting to note that when Lancelot appears in the *Lanzelet* of Ulrich von Zarzikhoven, no mention is made of the love affair between Lancelot and Guinevere, for in this Lancelot has three lovers and marries the third, Iblis. The French characterization of Sir Lancelot as portrayed in the works of Chrétien de Troyes has him behaving like a textbook lover who, in true troubadour fashion, venerates Guinevere with an intensity that is usually only ever exhibited by religious zealots. The intentions of Chrétien de Troyes in such a depiction of a Knight of the Round Table was to show secular chivalry and courtly love as the finest aspects of the aristocratic culture. This might not have been so important to writers from countries where life at court was not so pre-eminent, and thus writers from those countries chose to alter the life of Sir Lancelot and make him a more general figure.

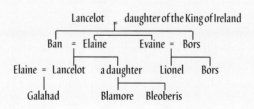

Lancelot's family tree (French sources)

Sir Lanval

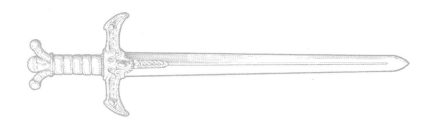

THE STORY OF SIR LANVAL is recounted several times, first of all in the twelfth-century *Lanval* by Marie de France (*fl.* 1160–90), and subsequently in English in the fourteenth-century *Sir Landeval* and in two sixteenth-century works, *Sir Lambewell* and *Sir Lambwell*. The son of a king from a distant, unnamed land, Lanval was well liked by his peers at the court for his beauty and prowess. A worthy knight of the Round Table, pure of heart and heavy of hand, he was greatly disliked by King Arthur for some reason that is never made clear.

One day Lanval decided to ride from the court unattended and enjoy the beauty of the day. After going a short distance, he came to a shallow river, but his horse could not be goaded into stepping into the water, so Lanval unbridled it and let it feed on the lush pasture. He then removed his cloak and lay down to sleep, but so troubled was he by the dislike of King Arthur and by the discomfort of the stony ground beneath him, that he tossed and turned on the grass. Some time later Lanval saw two fair maidens in the distance dressed in purple and carrying a beautiful golden bowl and a towel. When it became clear to Lanval that they were heading straight for him, he rose and made himself presentable.

The two maidens greeted the knight and told him that they had been sent by their mistress to fetch him, for she wished to speak with him. Lanval immediately agreed to go with them, as he could see their mistress's pavilion in the distance and was sure that she was of royal birth, for above the pavilion, which was made from silks of many different colours, there sat an eagle fashioned from gold, while the poles that held aloft the canopy were of finely spun gold.

Lanval entered the pavilion and saw the maiden lying on a couch that was more fine than anything he had ever seen before. The maiden beckoned him, so Lanval came forward and sat at her feet. She then told him that she had travelled from a distant land to pledge her love for him, eliciting from him a promise that he would tell no one of his love. Lanval readily agreed, for though he was happy among the other knights of the Round Table, he was saddened by the treatment of King Arthur and longed for the love of a maiden as beautiful as the one he sat looking at, a maiden whose beauty surpassed even that of Queen Guinevere. Lanval remained with the maiden for the remainder of the day, until the sun began to set in the west. She then told him that the time had come when they must part, but added that he had only to think of her and she would be with him, stressing that their meetings must always be in private and that if anyone discovered her existence it would mean that Lanval never saw her again. Sealing their pact with an embrace, Lanval made to leave, but was stopped by the two maidens who had brought him to the pavilion. They dressed him in clothes that even King Arthur would have been envious of, a fact that undoubtedly pleased Lanval no end. Leaving the pavilion, Lanval found his horse had been brought and tethered outside, and had been fitted with the most splendid saddle and bridle any man had ever seen.

All remained well for a long time, but even though Lanval was now one of the best dressed knights at court, he still did not attract the favour of the king. Then things took a disastrous turn. One evening, in the company of Sir Gawain and Sir Yvain, Sir Lanval was walking in the palace gardens when Guinevere and her entourage of ladies met with them. Sir Gawain and Sir Yvain gladly accepted the attentions of the ladies, but Sir Lanval, thinking of his love, pulled back and stood away from the party. Guinevere also made her way away from the throng, standing near to Sir Lanval, and pledged her undying love for him. Horrified, Lanval did not at first know how to respond, but when pressed by the queen, he told her that he could not betray the king by entering into an illicit union with the queen. Hot with rage, she then accused him of despising all women, for he had never been seen at court in the company of anyone other than his fellow knights.

Again Lanval was at a loss to know what to say, but finally retorted that he was in love and loved. However, when pressed by Guinevere, he would not tell her the name of the maiden he spoke of. Guinevere immediately planned her revenge, and when Arthur came to her chamber that night she unashamedly lied that Lanval had attempted to seduce her, but that she would have nothing to do with him. She then added, for spite, that Lanval had spoken of a women he loved whose meekest serving wench was more finely dressed and smiled more sweetly than the queen.

Furious, Arthur called for Lanval to explain himself, but knowing that by speaking of his love to Guinevere he had lost the maiden for ever, all Lanval could do was slowly recount exactly what had passed between himself and Guinevere. Arthur refused to believe Sir Lanval and called for him to be tried by his peers at a future date, only agreeing to release him after Sir Gawain had pledged all his lands as surety.

On the day of his hearing, Lanval was brought before the entire company to answer Arthur's charge of treason. The Duke of Cornwall, who remains unnamed, spoke on Lanval's behalf, saying that even though King Arthur thought ill of Sir Lanval, none of the others at the court did and that if he were found guilty, he should be banished rather than executed. As all the other knights swiftly agreed to this, Arthur could do nothing but concur, though this agreement served only to anger Guinevere further. The Duke of Cornwall then spoke to Lanval, urging him to bring his lady forward so that the charge brought against him could be dropped. Lanval said he could not and nor would he name her. However, just as the knights were about to deliver their verdict, two fair maidens entered the great hall and approached Arthur. Seeing them, the Duke of Cornwall asked Lanval if either was the lady he loved. Lanval replied that he had never set eyes on them before.

When the ladies had been greeted by Arthur, they spoke to him and requested lodgings for themselves and for their lady, who would shortly arrive. Arthur agreed and then turned back to his knights, who had risen when the ladies entered the hall but had now returned to consider their verdict. Again, as the Duke of Cornwall rose to deliver the verdict of the knights, two more ladies entered the hall, these two being more lovely and more finely dressed than the previous pair. Again Lanval could only answer that he had never set eyes on either before when asked if one was his love.

Once more the knights reassembled to deliver their verdict on Sir Lanval, and once again, as the Duke of Cornwall rose, the proceedings came to a halt when a commotion was heard outside. Towards the castle, astride a pure-white horse, came a maiden the like of whom no one had ever seen before. As she made her way to the castle, the people pressed forward to see her, for her beauty far exceeded that of even Guinevere. When Sir Gawain saw the maiden he rushed to Sir Lanval, who, hearing Gawain's description, knew that this lady was the one he loved.

The lady entered the hall and approached Arthur, who stepped down from his seat to greet her. Looking around, she saw Sir Lanval and then spoke to King Arthur, saying that she loved Sir Lanval and that Sir Lanval loved her. She then chided the king for his dislike of Sir Lanval and for the treachery of Guinevere, calling on the knights to decide the quarrel between herself and the queen. As none of them could deny that Sir Lanval was telling the truth, Arthur asked forgiveness of Sir Lanval, which he gladly gave. Guinevere simply sat stony-faced and would say nothing. Shortly afterwards, the entire company gathered as the lady – named by some as Tryamour – and Sir Lanval mounted the pure white horse – called Blanchard in some sources – and left, never to be seen again. The Bretons say that they travelled to Avalon and still live there in happiness and peace to this very day.[1]

Although Lanval is clearly a later addition to the Knights of the Round Table, his story vividly illustrates the way in which a knight would be bound to keep a promise, even though, as here, that promise might ultimately lead to his banishment or even his death. Lanval's love has little to do with courtliness or chivalry, but rather the action is between magic and everyday life, and between the pitfalls of court life and the world of beautiful supernatural beings.

Merlin

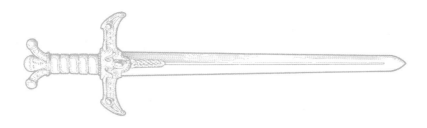

THE MOST FAMOUS WIZARD OF ALL TIMES and Arthur's counsellor, Merlin guided the young king at the start of his reign, though later the king did not always follow the advice given to him. We know of Merlin by that name simply because the Latinized form of his Welsh name, Myrddin, would be Merdinus, and that would unfortunately have connected it with the Latin word *merdus* – 'dung'. Merlin is not a personal name, but rather a place name, Myrddin originating in the Celtic Maridunon, Carmarthen, which in Welsh is Caerfyrddin. It would seem that the wizard was so called because he originated from there. At least, Geoffrey of Monmouth thought so, and although other sources agree in principle, they say that the town was founded by him and therefore named after him. Robert de Boron says he was born in Brittany, but this is commonly regarded as an attempt by that author to claim Merlin for the author's own country of birth.

Many stories abound about the birth of Merlin, but usually he is said to have been the offspring of an incubus (a demon believed in folk-lore to have sexual intercourse with sleeping women) and a nun, set on earth by the devils of hell, who were determined to counterbalance the good introduced by Jesus Christ. However, their plans went awry when their intended evil being was baptized. This is not by any means the only account of his birth, but does appear to predate all others. In Welsh tradition his mother was called Aldan, a historical daughter of a south Wales nobleman; whether she was a nun is unclear. French romance calls her Optima – a name that also sometimes appears in Welsh sources – while Pieri's fourteenth-century *Storia di Merlino* names her as Marinaia. The Elizabethan play *Birth of Arthur*[1] calls her Joan go-to-'t. Welsh tradition further contradicts Merlin's supposed lack of a father by giving him the paternal pedigree shown right. His father, named

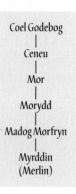

Coel Godebog
|
Ceneu
|
Mor
|
Morydd
|
Madog Morfryn
|
Myrddin
(Merlin)

as Madog Morfryn in this genealogy, was also said to have been Morgan Frych, claimed by some to have been a prince of Gwynedd, thus making Merlin of royal blood. Geoffrey of Monmouth made him the King of Powys, and the idea that Merlin was of royal stock is found in *Venetia edificia* (1624) by Strozzi.

Merlin's story, including his connection with the Arthurian legends, begins long before the birth of the king he was to advise and whose downfall he so rightly prophesied. While still a youth he became connected with Vortigern, the King of Britain some time after the end of the Roman occupation.[2] Vortigern was attempting to erect a tower on Dinas Emrys,[3] but with little success, for every time he built it up, it promptly fell down again. His counsellors told him that it would be necessary to sacrifice a fatherless child in order to rectify the problem, and, as these were hardly thick on the ground, the alleged son of the incubus, Merlin, now a youth, was picked. When brought to the site of the tower, Merlin told Vortigern that the problem lay beneath the ground in the form of two dragons hidden in an underground lake. Excavation of the site proved this to be the case (subsequent archaeological excavation has revealed an underground pool), and two dragons, one red and one white, emerged, causing Merlin to utter a series of prophecies, one of which was that Vortigern would be burned to death in his tower, a prophecy that came true when he was defeated by Ambrosius Aurelius.[4] The story of the two battling dragons, and how they came to be imprisoned beneath Dinas Emrys, is found in the *Mabinogion* story of *Llud and Llefelys*.[5]

There seems to be an unrecorded gap in Merlin's life at this point, for he next appears when Ambrosius Aurelius defeated Vortigern and wished to erect a monument both to his success and to commemorate the dead. Merlin advised him to go to Ireland and bring back from Mount Killaraus certain stones that formed the Giants' Ring. This was done and they were erected on Salisbury Plain, today being better known as Stonehenge, though this legend takes no account whatever of the actual history of Stonehenge. Following the death of Ambrosius Aurelius, Uther ascended to the throne, but during a war with Gorlois, he became infatuated with Gorlois's wife, Igraine. One of Uther's men (Ulfin Ridcaradoch, according to Geoffrey of Monmouth, but otherwise known as Ulfius, Urfin or Ursin) suggested they consult Merlin and ask for his help. When they did so, Merlin consented to enable Uther to lie with Igraine on the proviso that any child born of the union should be entrusted to him to raise. Uther agreed, and Merlin altered the king's appearance so that he resembled Gorlois. On the night that Uther lay with Igraine, accompanied by Ulfius, who had been transformed into the likeness of Brastias, one of Gorlois's knights, Gorlois was killed in battle. When the child was born, Merlin appeared and took him away, as had been agreed, placing him with Ector. This child was the infant Arthur. Uther married Igraine, but two years later he died. The country was again thrown into disarray, for there was no worthy successor to the throne – a situation that was to continue for 13 years after Uther's death.

Meanwhile, the young Arthur was raised by Ector, unaware of his parentage or destiny. When aged just 15 he accompanied his foster father and Kay, Ector's son, to a tournament in London, acting as Kay's squire. However, when they arrived Arthur found to his horror that he had forgotten Kay's sword. Remembering that he had seen one embedded in a rock some distance away, he went to fetch it. Arthur easily removed the sword from the stone, a test devised by Merlin to find the next true king, and hurried back to the tournament. Kay recognized the sword that so many had tried to remove but none had been able to, and tried to make his father believe that he had removed it himself. However, Ector prevailed upon his son to tell the truth, fully realizing what the sword signified, and Kay owned up. Arthur once more drew out the sword, this time in public, and was duly proclaimed king. This story is told more fully in the profile for Sir Kay (see pages 107–10).

Events after the crowning of King Arthur differ according to source, some even attributing the manufacture of the Round Table to Merlin. In the early days of Arthur's reign Merlin remains in the background, acting almost solely as the king's adviser. A prime example of this prophetic advice was when Arthur wanted to marry Guinevere: Merlin advised against it, saying that she would be unfaithful to him and would ultimately bring about the destruction of his realm, leading to his death. Arthur none the less ignored the advice of his counsellor.

According to Sir Thomas Malory, Merlin became infatuated with the Lady of the Lake, called Nimue by Malory but referred to as Viviane or Vivienne elsewhere. He taught her his magical secrets, but she turned these against him and imprisoned him in a cave or an oak tree. The spell that holds him there can be broken only when Arthur once again rules.

Geoffrey of Monmouth and earlier Welsh sources say that Merlin was still in circulation following the battle of Camlann, being one of those aboard the barge, along with the bard Taliesin and the ferryman Barinthus, an obscure early Celtic sea deity, that brought the dying king to Avalon to be healed of his deadly wound by the goddess Morgan Le Fay, shape-changing mistress of therapy, music and the arts, co-ruling with her eight sisters. With the kingdom in disarray, Merlin went mad following the battle of Arthuret[6] and took to living as a wild man in the woods. One source, the Norman-Welsh chronicler and ecclesiastic Giraldus Cambrensis (c.1146-c.1223), explains Merlin's loss of sanity by saying that it followed his beholding some horrible sight in the sky, a bad omen, during the fighting, in which he had been on the side of Rhydderch Hael, King of Cumbria and husband of Merlin's twin sister, Ganieda.[7] Three of Merlin's brothers were also reputed to have been killed during the battle, though their names are not given and remain a mystery.

After a while, Ganieda persuaded Merlin to give up his wild life in the woods and return to civilization, but upon his return he revealed to Rhydderch Hael that Ganieda had been unfaithful to him. Once again madness took hold of him and he returned to the forest, urging his wife, the flower maiden Guendoloena,[8] to re-marry, apparently divorcing her in order to free her. She agreed but, in his madness, Merlin arrived at the wedding riding a stag and leading a herd of deer (clearly a reworking of an earlier pagan tradition). In his rage, forgetting that it was he who had urged his wife to remarry, he tore the antlers from the stag and hurled them at the bridegroom, who remains unnamed, and killed him. He returned to the forest once more, where Ganieda built him an observatory from which he could study the stars.

Welsh poetic sources that are considerably earlier in date than the writings of Geoffrey of Monmouth largely agree with his account (they are obviously his sources), though they state that Merlin fought against Rhydderch Hael rather than for him. Similar tales are told in Welsh tradition regarding a character by the name of Lailoken, who was in the service of Rhydderch Hael, and it would appear that this caused Geoffrey of Monmouth to change Merlin's allegiance. Lailoken is similar to the Welsh word meaning 'twin brother' and, as Merlin and Ganieda were thought to be twins, this may have simply been a nickname for Merlin himself, though, as has already been said, Merlin is not actually a personal name.

Many other legends and tales surround the character of Merlin. He was said to have saved the baby Tristan and to have had a daughter named La Damosel del Grant Pui de Mont Dolerous; it was also said that he was not imprisoned by Nimue, but instead voluntarily retired to a place of confinement to live out the remainder of his days. This last option seems to have some connection with the story of Ganieda building him an observatory in the forest, for that would have been a splendid place for the wizard to spend his final years.

Geoffrey of Monmouth appears to draw further on earlier Welsh sources when he connects Merlin with Taliesin, a character with whom he seems to be inexorably intertwined in the Welsh mind. One Welsh tradition says that Merlin was not just one but three incarnations of the same person, the first appearing in Vortigern's time, the second being as Taliesin himself, and the last Merlin, the wild man of the forests. This idea of a multiple Merlin is again found in the writings of the twelfth-century Norman-Welsh chronicler Giraldus Cambrensis, who says there were two, wizard and wild man. This theory doubtless springs from the impossibly long lifespan usually attributed to Merlin. Modern thinking even had him reincarnated once more as Nostradamus, the Latinized form of Michel de Notredame, the sixteenth century prophet (1503–66). This idea has not found popular support, though, and is now almost universally disregarded.

The legends of Merlin are not confined to British and Breton tradition. The Italian romances also add a great deal to his story, stating, in one instance, that he was unsuccessfully charged with heresy by a bishop named Conrad, who lived to regret his accusation, and that he uttered prophecies about the House of Hohenstaufen.[9] An Italian poet, Matteo Maria Boiardo (1434–94), mixes Merlin into the story of Tristan and Iseult, saying that Merlin created a fountain of forgetfulness for Tristan to drink from and thus forget Iseult, but Tristan never found it. Ludovico Ariosto (1474–1533) says that his soul lives on in a tomb, and that it informed Bradmante, a female warrior of the Carolingian era (751–987), that the house of Este[10] would be descended from her. Strozzi further adds that when Attila the Hun (c.406–53)[11] invaded Italy, Merlin lived in a cave and, while there, invented the telescope which may be another reference to Ganieda's observatory.

His death is as clouded in legend as was his life. One Welsh tradition says that he was held captive by a scheming woman in a cave on Bryn Myrddin near Carmarthen, a location shown on Ordnance Survey maps as Merlin's Hill. This seems to echo the story of his being held captive by Nimue. Some say that if you listen in the twilight you can still hear his groans and the clanking of the iron chains that bind him, while others say that the noise is him still working away in his underground prison. His place of confinement is sometimes said to be a cave in the park of Dynevor Castle, Dyfed, in the vicinity of Llandeilo. It is also claimed that he died and was buried on Bardsey Island,[12] while Breton tradition has him spellbound in whitethorn bushes in the woods of Bresilien in Brittany.

The Welsh *Trioedd Ynys Prydein* (commonly referred to as the 'Triads'), however, say that he put to sea in a house of glass and was never heard of again. On this voyage he took with him the Thirteen Treasures or Curiosities of Britain, which are most commonly listed as:

1. Llen Arthur – the veil of Arthur – which made the wearer invisible. This is sometimes referred to as the Mantle of Invisibility.
2. Dyrnwyn – the sword of Rhydderch Hael – which would burst into flame from the cross to the point if any man save Rhydderch Hael drew it.
3. Corn Brangaled – the horn of Brangaled – which provided any drink desired.
4. Cadair, neu car Morgan Mwynfawr – the chair or car of Morgan Mwynfawr – which would carry a person seated in it anywhere he wished to go.
5. Mwys Gwyddno – the hamper of Gwyddno – which had the power to turn any meat placed on it into sufficient to feed 100 people.
6. Hogalen Tudno – the whetstone of Tudno Tudglyd – which would sharpen none but the weapon of a brave man.
7. Pais Padarn – the cloak of Padarn – which would make the wearer invisible.
8. Pair Drynog – the cauldron of Drynog – in which none but the meat of a brave man would boil.
9. Dysgyl a gren Rhydderch – the platter of Rhydderch – upon which any meat desired would appear.
10. Tawlbwrdd – a chess or rather backgammon board having a ground of gold and men of silver who would play themselves.
11. Mantell – a robe that would keep the wearer warm, no matter how severe the weather.
12. Modrwy Eluned – the ring of Eluned – which conferred invisibility on the wearer.
13. Cyllel Llawfrodedd – a Druid sacrificial knife.

It should be noted that these were by no means the only items numbered among the Thirteen Treasures that Merlin was said to have sailed away with, but they are the most common in Welsh tradition.

Modern times have not entirely forgotten Merlin either. Yearly pilgrimages continued to Merlin's Spring at Barenton, Brittany, until they were stopped by the Vatican in 1853. His ghost is still said to haunt Merlin's Cave at Tintagel, while the wizard himself is said to be buried in almost as many locations as Arthur. These include Drumelzier in Scotland, under Merlin's Mount in the grounds of Marlborough College (the town's coat of arms bears the motto *Ubi nunc sapientis ossa Merlini* – 'Where are the bones of Merlin now?'), at Mynydd Fyrddin in Wales and in Merlin's Hill Cave near Carmarthen.

Merlin's historicity is now thought to be without doubt, but he was not the mythologized wizard of the Arthurian legends. There were in fact two Merlin's alive during the time of Vortigern and Arthur. One was called Myrddin Wyllt and lived in Scotland, but it is Myrddin Emrys, born and raised in Carmarthen, who has become the Arthurian Merlin. It is generally believed that he must have been a man of very high intelligence, with extremely advanced knowledge for his time, when magic was simply another name for scientific expertise. He may have been, as has been suggested, a latter-day Druid who took part in shamanistic rituals, but many attempts have also been made to link Merlin with earlier Celtic deities.

One theory states that he represented the morning star, while his sister, Ganieda, was the evening star. He may indeed have been a deity, for the Welsh 'Triads' indicate that he had territorial rights as a god over Britain; in this work the earliest name for Britain is said to have been Merlin's Precinct. However, the truth behind this is probably that the prophet became connected with an earlier deity and took on many of his attributes, such were his astonishing powers. To the peasants of his time, his wisdom and foresight must have seemed very godly indeed. Other attempts have been made to connect him with the god Mabon, Celtic god of liberation, harmony, unity and music, or, through his association with stags, with Cernunnos, the Celtic horned god. Many theories have been put forward, but the truth of the matter, as with so much of Arthurian legend, may never be known.

There are countless prophecies attributed to Merlin, some of which appear to have been strangely fulfilled, while others may well be fulfilled in the future. In the Vale of Twy near Abergwili there stands a large stone in a field. Many years ago a young man was killed while digging under this stone for buried treasure, it being a popular belief at the time that such stones marked the sites of buried treasures beyond belief. Myrddin had prophesied that one day a raven would drink the blood of a man from this stone. Whether or not a raven actually did so is not known, but the prophecy seems to have come true.

The most famous prophecies attributed to Merlin were those relating to the town of Carmarthen:

Llanllwch a fu,
Caerfyrddu a sud,
Abergwili a saif.

Llanllwch has been,
Carmarthen shall sink,
Abergwili shall stand.

and

Caerfyrddin, cei oer fore,
Daerr a'th lwnc, dwr i'th le.

Carmarthen, thou shalt have a cold morning,
Earth shall swallow thee, water into thy place.

There are still old folk living there who await the catastrophe that they believe will one day befall their town. At the end of one street there used to stand an ancient and withered oak tree known as Merlin's Tree or the Priory Oak. Every care was taken over the centuries to protect it from falling, for Merlin had prophesied that when it did Carmarthen would fall. However, in 1978 the local authority decided to risk the prophecy and remove the tree, which had become a hazard to the town's traffic and consisted mainly of concrete and iron bars anyway. Today it is to be found in the foyer of St Peter's Civic Hall, which might explain why catastrophe has not yet befallen, for the tree has simply been moved and is therefore still within the town and protecting it.

Merlin also prophesied that Carmarthen would sink when Llyn Eiddwen, a lake in Dyfed, dried up and that one day a bull would go to the very top of the tower of St Peter's Church in Carmarthen – this latter strange prophesy was actually fulfilled by a calf.

Although Merlin may not exactly be a 'hero' of the Round Table, he is an essential part of the legends that surround it. In fact, some sources actually attribute its manufacture to Merlin. When Merlin's long lifespan is taken into account, perhaps these sources are telling the truth. The Round Table may indeed have been the Old Table of King Uther Pendragon. As Merlin was also Uther's adviser, it seems reasonable to suggest that Merlin manufactured the table for Uther but, before it could be used, Uther died and the table passed into the custodianship of King Leodegrance, from whom it later passed to Arthur, who finally put it to the use Merlin had originally intended.

No matter what the truth, Merlin remains the single most enigmatic character at King Arthur's court and would have had some part, no matter how small, in determining the fates of Arthur, his knights and the Round Table itself.

Sir Mordred

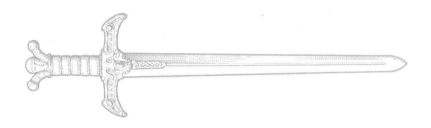

THE INCEST-BEGOTTEN 'NEPHEW' OF ARTHUR, or the son of Lot, who usurped the throne after Arthur had left him as his regent when he undertook his Continental campaign, Sir Mordred is perhaps the darkest member of the court of King Arthur. His character develops progressively through the Arthurian cycle, until he becomes the epitome of evil and the cause of the destruction of Arthur and his noble court.

Early writers seem quite content with the fact that, because of his relationship to the king, Mordred harboured a grudge that was to lead him into war against his father, whose throne he coveted, a war that was to cost him his own life and destroy all the good that King Arthur had ever done. Mordred is almost always depicted dressed from head to foot in black, an ideal Black Knight, and usually in the company of the equally evil and scheming Morgan Le Fay, the half-sister of Arthur. It has even been suggested that Mordred became the protégé of Morgan Le Fay and was simply doing her bidding when he set out to destroy his father and take over the throne.

It seems entirely appropriate, therefore, that it should have been Mordred who was the first to bring news of the adultery of Lancelot and Guinevere to the attention of King Arthur, though the news was initially received with little credence by the king. Mordred thus set out to trap the knight and the queen together and bring conclusive evidence to Arthur. By destroying the king's heart, he knew that he could destroy the Round Table, for the loyalties of the knights would be split between Arthur and Lancelot. Mordred, Agravain and 12 other knights, therefore, lay in wait for their chance, which was not long in presenting itself.

On the now infamous occasion when Lancelot visited Guinevere in her bedchamber, it was Mordred who led the party that discovered the two lovers together, but he got a great deal more than he bargained for. Mordred had assumed that he would be able to take Lancelot quite easily, even though he secretly longed to kill that virtuous knight, but this was not to be. Unarmed as he was, Sir Lancelot proved to be at his most dangerous when cornered, and he killed all those who sought to expose his affair with the queen, save, perhaps a little unluckily for him, Sir Mordred, who barely escaped with his life and crept back to Arthur to tell him what had happened.

The death of so many knights at the hands of Lancelot was to do two things. First, it proved to the king that the adultery that he had hoped beyond hope was false was in fact true, but, more importantly, it ensured that many of the other knights were openly hostile to Lancelot, none more so, perhaps, than Sir Gawain, whose brother Agravain was one of the first to be killed.

Guinevere was condemned to be burned at the stake for treason, but was rescued, moments before the fire was kindled, by Sir Lancelot, who killed a great many of the other Knights of the Round Table in the course of the rescue, Sir Bors and Sir Gareth among them. Even now King Arthur wanted nothing more than the return of Guinevere and peace with his old friend Lancelot, but he unwisely took the counsel of Sir Mordred, who persuaded him to travel to France and lay siege to Lancelot's castle, Joyous Gard (note that various authorities have identified Joyous Gard with the castle at Bamburgh, Northumberland).

With Arthur and most of the court overseas, Mordred faked news of Arthur's death, had himself proclaimed king and said that he would take as his wife Guinevere, who had been allowed safe passage home from France, her cause having been championed by Lancelot. She took herself off to London and barricaded herself in the Tower of London, laying in sufficient provisions for a long siege.[1] News finally reached Arthur of his nephew's treachery, and Mordred was duly defeated by Arthur on his return at the battle of Richborough. Arthur pursued him and his fleeing army. Mordred was once more defeated at Winchester, where some sources say Gawain met his death, before both armies pushed on into Cornwall, where they met for the third and final battle at Camlann. Even though Arthur had sought to make peace with his treacherous nephew, some saying that he was advised to do so by the ghost of Sir Gawain, this was not to be, as during the peace negotiations an unnamed knight drew his sword to kill an adder that had bitten his ankle. Both sides saw the glint of metal in the sun and, amidst shouts of treachery, battle recommenced. As the fighting died down Arthur, in the company of Sir Bedivere and his brother Sir Lucan, spied Mordred leaning on his sword among a great pile of bodies. Arthur called for his lance, though both Bedivere and Lucan tried to stop him, and rushed at Mordred, running him through. As Mordred fell, his sword flew from his hand and struck Arthur a mortal blow. The king was taken off to the Isle of Avalon so that his mortal wounds might be healed. This was reported to have taken place in the year 542. The French *Ly Myreur des*

Histoires claimed that Mordred survived the last battle, only to be subsequently defeated by Lancelot. This work also says that Lancelot executed Guinevere, believing she had complied with Mordred's plans, and incarcerated the living Mordred in the same tomb as the dead queen, Mordred cannibalizing Guinevere before dying of starvation.

The *Annales Cambriae* say that both Arthur and Medrawt (Mordred) perished at Camlann[2] but do not say that they were on opposing sides. This assertion does not come until later sources. Geoffrey of Monmouth says that Mordred was Arthur's nephew, the son of the king's sister, Anna, and her husband, Lot. The idea that Mordred was the offspring of an incestuous relationship appears only latterly, the earliest occurrence being in the *Mort Artu*, part of the French *Vulgate Version*. Sir Thomas Malory also carries on this theme, saying that Mordred was the result of a liaison between Arthur and his sister Morgause, though Arthur did not know they were related. When he discovered the truth, he attempted to kill Mordred by having all the children born on the same day as Mordred set adrift. Mordred was shipwrecked, but survived and was fostered and raised by Nabur, about whom nothing else is known. The *Mabinogion* story of the *Dream of Rhonabwy* makes Mordred Arthur's foster son as well as his nephew. Robert Wace (*c.*1115–83), in his *Roman de Brut*, makes Mordred the brother of Guinevere, whom Arthur had seized and made his queen. The *Alliterative Morte Arthure*, a 4,346-line Middle English poem dating from *c.*1400, further states that Mordred and Guinevere had a child.

As an adult, Mordred came to Arthur's court, was made a knight and was, for some time, the companion of Lancelot. When the ruling family of Orkney were in conflict with Pellinore, Mordred took their side in the battle and killed Lamorak, Pellinore's son. Early Welsh sources tend to portray Mordred as a heroic figure, rather than a villain, and Welsh tradition says he married Cywyllog, daughter of Caw, by whom he had two sons, one of whom was named Melehan and was killed by Sir Bors. However, the story that mentions his two sons is a fairly late addition to the Arthurian cycle, for it says that Melehan and his brother seized the kingdom after the death of their father.

If the medieval writers were looking for a scapegoat for the ultimate downfall of King Arthur, they could have found no more appropriate subject than the evil, scheming Sir Mordred. In their search for a clear-cut ending to the Arthurian story, they latched on to Sir Mordred and wove around him an elaborate tale of deception and betrayal that not only fulfilled their purposes but also, regrettably, damaged the persona of King Arthur and showed him as an easily led, and misled, figure.

Sir Morfran ab Tegid

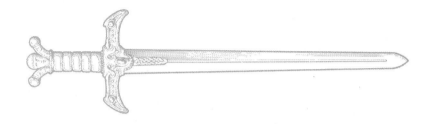

NAMED AS ONE OF THE TWENTY-FOUR KNIGHTS of King Arthur's Court, Morfran ab Tegid (Morfran 'son of Tegid') owes his origins to one of the earliest of all the Welsh myths, that of his mother Cerridwen and the birth of the bard Taliesin, though it does not actually much concern Morfran ab Tegid himself. It is, however, worth relating the legend at some length, since it is a perfect illustration of the concept of two opposing forces that is found so widely within the mythology and legends of the world.

Cerridwen is the corn goddess and wife of Tegid Voel, a man of gentle lineage who lived on an island in the middle of Lake Tegid. Some sources say that Tegid Voel actually means 'Old Man of [Lake] Tegid', though this must be treated with some scepticism. Cerridwen is usually represented as a crone, the goddess of dark and prophetic powers. Her totem animal was the sow, which was seen to represent the fecundity of the Otherworld, whose cauldron,[1] in which potions of inspiration and divine knowledge were brewed, was entrusted to her care.

Like many Celtic goddesses, Cerridwen had two opposing children. One was the maiden Crearwy, the most beautiful girl ever to have been born, her very person radiating light and warmth. The other was Morfran ab Tegid, sometimes better known by his nickname of Afagddu, the ugliest child ever to have lived, whose soul was dark and cold.

To compensate her son for his misfortune Cerridwen decided to employ the Otherworldly cauldron she kept and brew for him a potion that would empower him with the gifts of inspiration and knowledge, thus giving him the ability to know all things — past, present and future. Collecting together the magical herbs required, according to the books of Fferyllt,[2] she placed them in her cauldron and set Gwion Bach, the young son of Gwreang, to stir the potion for the required year and a day, and the blind man Morda to stoke the fire. At the end of the allotted time three drops of the hot liquid splashed on to Gwion Bach's thumb. As the little boy sucked his thumb to cool it he was filled with the potency of the brew. Having now given up its essence, the remainder of the potion became poisonous, the cauldron spilt asunder and the contents poisoned the local waterways and killed the horses of Gwyddno Garanhir,[3] which drank the contaminated water. The sucking of the thumb by Gwion Bach may enshrine an ancient Celtic divinatory practice that involved chewing the thumb. This practice, known in early Ireland as Imbas Forosnai, seems to have relied on the notion that chewing the raw flesh of the thumb imparted sagacity. It also parallels the story of Fionn mac Cumhaill, who sucked his thumb when it accidentally brushed the Salmon of Wisdom he was cooking for his master, an act that bestowed on him the same powers Gwion Bach found himself filled with.

Gwion Bach immediately knew that his life was in danger and fled the site. When Cerridwen found the cauldron in pieces, she flew into a rage and beat Morda so cruelly about the head with a billet of wood that one of his eyes fell out on to his cheek. Realizing that Gwion Bach was responsible for the loss of her potion, Cerridwen dashed off after the boy in the guise of a fearful black hag and soon started to gain on him. Seeing Cerridwen, Gwion Bach used his new-found powers to change himself into a hare so that he might run faster, but Cerridwen countered by changing herself into a greyhound. Gwion Bach saw Cerridwen gaining again and leapt into a river, changing into a fish as he did so. Cerridwen dived in after him and became an otter. Gwion Bach left the river and flew up into the air as a bird, with Cerridwen following as a hawk. Finally Gwion Bach sighted a barn and, dropping on to the threshing floor, turned himself into a grain of wheat, thinking that he would be safe among the thousands of other grains that lay scattered all around. Cerridwen changed herself into a hen and, scratching around the floor, swallowed the hapless Gwion Bach. This shape-changing frenzy appears to correspond to totem animals and the cycle of the seasons.

Resuming her human form, Cerridwen discovered that she was pregnant. Nine months later she gave birth to Gwion Bach as a boy so beautiful that she could not bring herself to kill him. Instead she sewed him up inside a leather bag and threw him into the river. The bag caught on the fish weir of Gwyddno Garanhir whose son Elphin found and opened it. The first thing he saw was the forehead of the child inside and he immediately exclaimed, 'Taliesin', thus naming the child, for Taliesin means 'Radiant Brow'.

Cerridwen, whose name means 'White Grain', was also known as Hên Wen, or 'old white one', the sow that supposedly gave birth to several monstrous offspring, one of which was the Cath Palug,[4] though this animal also has another tale of its birth (see below). She was the patroness of poetry, a just connection considering that the birth of the great bard Taliesin is a part of her story. She was, through her totem animal, connected with the sow goddess, as well as with Albine, the eponym of Albion, an archaic name still sometimes used to refer poetically to Britain. Cerridwen lived at Caer Siddi, also known as Caer Feddwidd or Caer Rigor,[5] an Otherworldly kingdom that was represented in the stars as a spiral, although this realm is also sometimes associated with Arianrhod.

Not content with all these attributes and associations, Cerridwen was also said to have been given a kitten that grew up to be the Cath Palug. This connection led Cerridwen to have associations with a cat cult, although, quite perversely, she also had connections with wolves and was said by some to have been the centre of a Neolithic[6] cult.

With such a complex mother, it is little wonder that Morfran later became connected with the Arthurian legends, for he would have been the half-brother of Taliesin, and thus of great importance to the early Welsh. Morfran does not appear widely within the core of the Arthurian cycle, but he seems to be a bridge between the early pagan Welsh beliefs and their later, post-Christian reincarnations.

An ideal example of this is with regard to the monstrous Cath Palug, the mythical animal that was the offspring of Hên Wen, which, as already stated, was another name for Cerridwen. This would mean that the Cath Palug was a relative of Morfran ab Tegid. How he felt, though, when Sir Kay travelled to Anglesey to do battle with the Cath Palug is, regrettably, not recorded. King Arthur himself was also said to have fought with another example of the Cath Palug, though this might be the same animal.

Morfran ab Tegid does feature in the battle of Camlann, Arthur's last battle, where it is recorded that no one dared to attack him because they all mistook him for a devil on account of his extreme ugliness. Here he is mentioned in parallel with Sir Sandav, who was so beautiful that no one dared strike him as they took him to be an angel. This again illustrates the reworking of the earlier pagan beliefs about opposing forces always appearing in unison. Morfran ab Tegid is, without doubt, a memory of the very earliest Arthurian traditions, and it seems only right that he should have survived through all the various retellings at the hands of a great many writers and pseudo-historians. As Arthur was to be elevated to an almost godly status, it is appropriate that he should have alongside him the son of a goddess, for this seems to further confer the status of a deity on Arthur himself, since no mortal man would dare to demand the services of a divine being so freely.

Sir Perceval

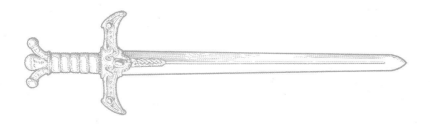

PERCEVAL IS THE NAME OF TWO CHARACTERS from the Arthurian legends. The first was the father of Sir Perceval, according to the fourteenth-century English romance *Sir Perceval of Galles*. He had apparently been killed, some years before Perceval became aware of his identity, by a Red Knight whom his son subsequently killed.

The main Sir Perceval was known among Welsh sources as Peredur. The name Perceval appears to have been the invention of Chrétien de Troyes, for the earliest reference to a character by this name is in his *Le conte de graal*, a work that is sometimes referred to as *Perceval*. In German sources he is called Parsifal or Parzival, the German writers such as Gottfried von Strassburg taking the earlier French texts and elaborating on them, often using their own personal experiences of court life.

Raised in the woods by his unnamed mother, for she wanted him to know nothing of knighthood, he saw some of Arthur's knights and was determined to go to court and become one. His mother, unable to convince him otherwise, dressed him in fool's clothes and told him to demand either a kiss or a jewel from any lady he should meet. When Perceval came across a lady asleep in a tent, he kissed her and purloined her ring. On his arrival at Arthur's court he heard that a Red Knight, the killer of his father, had absconded with a valuable cup. He pursued him after being taunted by Sir Kay and killed the knight, afterwards staying with Gornemant de Goort, an elderly knight, the prince of the unidentified realm of Graherz, who taught him chivalry and knighted him in the hope that Perceval would marry his daughter Liaze, although his plans did not come to fruition. Perceval returned to Arthur's court and became one of the Knights of the Round Table, leaving again to undertake the quest for the Holy Grail. During this quest he was set upon by a large number of thieves and was close to losing his life when another knight appeared and put the thieves to flight. This knight was Sir Galahad, whom Perceval failed to recognize, as Galahad had left Arthur's court carrying a white shield and now bore a red one. As Sir Galahad gave chase to the fleeing thieves, Sir Perceval sat down, for his own horse had been killed during the fight.

As he sat there a knight passed him at full gallop on a black horse, followed a short while later by a yeoman on a hackney (a breed of high-stepping carriage horse), who told Sir Perceval that the knight he had seen had stolen his master's horse, and he would be killed if he could not recover it. Sir Perceval mounted the hackney and gave chase, finally catching up with the knight, who killed the hackney and rode away. Dusting himself off, Sir Perceval called after the knight to stand and fight him on foot, but the knight simply rode away, leaving Perceval alone in the forest. Bewailing the misfortune that had befallen him, Sir Perceval settled down to sleep. At midnight he was awoken by a maiden who told him that she would lend him her own horse if he promised to come to her aid whenever she called on him. Perceval readily agreed and the lady left, only to return a short while later with the most magnificent black horse Perceval had ever laid eyes on.

Mounting the horse, Perceval was astonished by its speed, for within an hour, he had been carried the same distance a normal horse could have travelled at full gallop over four days. At the edge of a lake, Perceval reined the horse. The lake seemed to boil before his eyes, so he crossed himself at which the horse threw him off and changed into a foul fiend, which slithered away into the lake. Having given praise to God for his deliverance, Perceval explored the strange land he found himself in and soon came across a lion doing battle with a large serpent.

Sir Perceval quickly disposed of the serpent, upon which the lion roared gladly and fawned about Sir Perceval as a dog might with his master. The lion departed a short while later, but returned as night fell and that night slept with Sir Perceval to protect him from any harm. A short time later he arrived at the castle of Blanchefleur, which was being besieged by King Clamadeus, who desired the maiden for himself. Blanchefleur was prepared to kill herself rather than fall into the hands of Clamadeus. Perceval became her lover after successfully defeating King Clamadeus in single combat.

Desiring to visit his mother, Perceval was directed by a fisherman to a castle where he beheld the Grail procession,[1] saw a man reclining on a couch and was given a sword. However, Perceval failed to ask the Grail question,[2] and next morning, when he awoke, he found the castle deserted and only just managed to escape from it. The sword he had been given had fragmented. Encountering his cousin, who told him that he should have asked the Grail question, he took the sword to Trebuchet, who had originally made it and now repaired it.[3] *En route* Perceval was challenged by the husband of the lady he had encountered in the tent and from whom he had stolen the kiss and the jewel. He had misunderstood that Perceval had acted in innocence, and was overcome by the latter. Perceval was then said to have forgotten about God for a total of five years, but his uncle, the Hermit King, named as either Elyas Anais or King Pelles, absolved him.

This is as much as Chrétien de Troyes tells us, for his work is unfinished. However, in his *Continuation* Manessier takes up the story and tells how Perceval returned to the castle and asked the appropriate Grail question. He discovered that the Fisher King[4] had been wounded by fragments from a sword that had been used by Partinal to kill Goon Desert, the Fisher King's brother. Discovering that the wounds would not heal until the murderer had been dealt with, Perceval sought him out and killed him. The Fisher King was healed and his lands restored to fertility. Some sources add that the sword that had fragmented was the one manufactured by Trebuchet, and its repair, along with the disposal of Partinal, was required to break the curse of the Fisher King. Perceval's identity was then revealed to him as the nephew of the Grail King, who had been sustained by the Grail during his incapacity and when that king died, Perceval succeeded him, though upon successfully achieving the Grail, after which Galahad died, Perceval was said to have lived on for at least a year.

From these origins, Perceval subsequently appeared in romances on both sides of the English Channel. The English verse romance *Sir Perceval of Galles* says that his mother was Acheflour, the sister of Arthur, and his father, also called Perceval, had been killed many years previously by a Red Knight. His lover was called Lufamour in this work. Perceval was said to have died while away on a holy Crusade. The *Didot Perceval*[5] says that the Rich Fisher (another term for the Fisher King) revealed to Perceval the secret words that Jesus had passed on to Joseph of Arimathea. In *Peredur*, the Welsh variation of his story that forms a part of the *Mabinogion*, his father is named as Efrawg. Perceval is also named in this work as one of the cousins, the other being Gwrgi, of the British prince Gwenddoleu, against whom was fought the battle of Arfderydd, the battle fought *c.*575 for a 'lark's nest' (see page 182). The Grail procession is described as having included a maiden carrying a salver on which there was a head surrounded by blood. This head, Perceval later found out, was that of his cousin, whose death he had to avenge. It was in this version of Perceval's story that he was said to have done battle with an *afanc*.[6]

In the later *Queste del Sainte Graal*[7] and in the works of Sir Thomas Malory Perceval has to some degree become supplanted by Galahad, though it was he who was at first thought to have achieved the Grail. Malory calls Perceval's father Pellinore. Wolfram von Eschenbach makes his father Gahmuret, his mother Herzeloyde, the Queen of Wales and Northgalis,[8] and his sister Dindrane, who accompanied him on the quest for the Holy Grail but died after she voluntarily gave her blood to cure the leprous mistress of a castle the questers came to. Perceval's sons are named as Kardiez and Lohengrin The thirteenth-century French *Perlesvaus* again differs, making his father Julain and

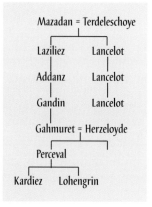

Descent of Perceval (according to Wolfram von Eschenbach)

his mother Yglais, the latter being a niece of Joseph of Arimathea. Gerbert, in his thirteenth century *Continuation* to the *Perceval* of Chrétien de Troyes, makes them Gales li Caus and Philosophine. The French *Bliocadran* makes his father the eponymous hero of that work, while the fourteenth century Italian *Tavola ritonda* makes his sister Agrestizia.

The German writers added much to the earlier romances concerning Perceval, but these adventures have little to do with the original character and have been added by the various authors, Gottfried von Strassburg and Wolfram von Eschenbach in particular, only to give the character of Perceval a more Teutonic nature. However, despite the attempts of these later writers to make Perceval the ideal of a Germanic knight, he remains essentially British, the pre-eminent knight at Arthur's court, representing spiritual chivalry, thus offsetting Sir Gawain, who was the pre-eminent representation of secular chivalry.

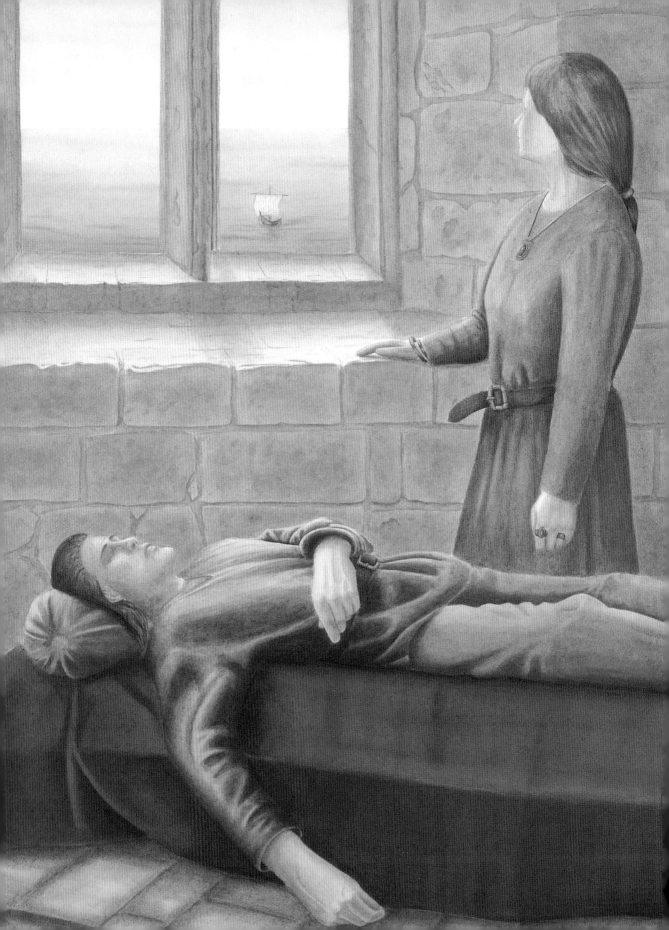

Sir Tristan

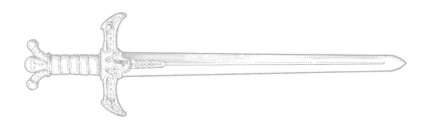

THE MOST TRAGIC OF ALL the Arthurian heroes, Tristan was a contemporary of Arthur, the nephew and champion of the possibly historical King Mark of Cornwall and also a Knight of the Round Table. Most romancers give some account of his story, but there is a wide diversity in his lineage.

The earliest surviving fragments of any poem concerning Tristan are by Thomas, a Norman poet who wrote at the Plantagenet court some time after 1150. Marie de France mentioned Tristan as an ideal lover in the 1160s, while Eilhart von Oberge wrote about him *c.*1170, followed by Béroul, another Norman poet, *c.*1190.

According to Sir Thomas Malory, the most widely quoted commentator, he was the son of Meliodas and Elizabeth, his relationship to Mark being as below:

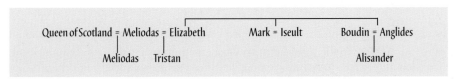

The Italian romance *Tristano Riccardiano* virtually echoes this, giving a very slightly different name to his mother, but naming his paternal grandfather as Felix. In this case Tristan's family tree resembles:

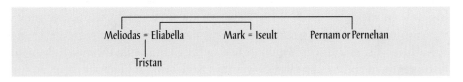

Gottfried von Strassburg differs quite markedly in his *Tristan and Isolde* (*c.*1210), the courtly epic written in Middle High German and based on an earlier version by the Anglo-Norman poet Thomas. In this version, Gottfried gives Rivalin and Blanchefleur as Tristan's parents, Blanchefleur being Mark's sister. Some sources replace Rivalin with King Rouland of Erminia.

Rivalin = Blanchefleur   Mark = Iseult
         |
       Tristan

Tristan's story is basically as follows.

He was the son of King Meliodas, King of Liones, and Elizabeth, and sister of King Mark of Cornwall, who died in childbirth. As a young man he entered the service of his uncle, King Mark, and was raised by Gorvenal,[1] who taught him all the skills of a knight. However, when King Mark refused to pay the customary tribute of 300 youths and 300 maidens to Ireland, Tristan championed his uncle and killed Morholt,[2] the giant Irish champion and brother of the Irish queen.

However, during the combat Tristan received a poisoned wound and, being advised that he could be cured only in Ireland, he returned there, quite wisely under an assumed name, which was either Tantris (a simple anagram of Tristan) or Pro of Iernsetir, his wound being cured by Iseult, the daughter of King Anguish.

When Tristan returned to Cornwall, he told his uncle of the beauty of Iseult, and so taken was the king with his description that he sent Tristan back to Ireland to woo Iseult on his behalf. King Anguish agreed to the marriage and Tristan set off to bring Iseult back to his uncle.[3] However, on the ship that carried them across the Irish Sea, he and Iseult mistakenly drank a love potion that Iseult's maid Brangien had hidden and that had been intended for Mark and his bride-to-be. Falling helplessly in love with each other, they embarked on their ill-fated love affair. On Iseult's wedding night she had her maid Brangien take her place under cover of darkness, so that Mark would not know she had already lain with Tristan. Iseult subsequently tried to have Brangien murdered to ensure her silence, but the attempt was unsuccessful and Iseult later repented of it.

Their affair continued undiscovered, though on one occasion King Mark and his adviser Melot, a dwarf who came from Aquitaine, hid in an orchard where Melot knew the two lovers met after dark. However, there was a full moon that night and Tristan, having arrived first, saw the shadows of Mark and Melot coming from the tree beneath which he stood. When he saw Iseult approaching, he did not move, thus putting Iseult on her guard. She too saw the shadows and concocted a story about how Tristan had sent her a note asking her to meet him there so they could discuss how to correct the false stories that were being told about them. Above

Tristan, Mark listened without moving a muscle and after the two lovers had gone their separate ways, he scolded Melot for spreading such falsehoods. The following day Mark publicly apologized to both Iseult and Tristan for ever having considered that the lies might have been true.

However, it was not long before the rumours once more started, so Mark's advisers Melot and Marjoduc, befriended Tristan in the hope of extracting some snippet of information, Marjoduc had originally been a true friend to Tristan but turned against him when he learned of the affair. Tristan was too clever for them and duly warned Iseult to be on her guard. Melot then devised a plan that he knew would catch out Sir Tristan and Iseult. On the day in question King Mark had himself bled along with Iseult and Tristan. That night he arranged it so that Tristan was to lodge in their quarters before going to the church to celebrate Mass. Before leaving, however, Mark had Melot sprinkled flour on the floor between Tristan and Iseult's respective beds, and had had the candles shrouded so there was only a little light in the room.

Sure enough, shortly after Mark had left, Tristan rose and made his way to Iseult's bed, but saw the flour and leapt across it. However, he landed awkwardly on Iseult's bed, causing the vein that had been opened when he had been bled once again to bleed freely. Wasting no time, Tristan returned to his own bed, but the damage had already been done, for when Mark returned and found Iseult's bed covered in blood, as well as Tristan's, he could draw only one conclusion, even though Iseult protected Tristan by making her own wound bleed before Mark returned.

Iseult was, however, very anxious to dispel any lingering suspicion and so undertook to swear on a hot iron that she was not an adulteress. When the time came, Iseult fell into the arms of a beggar (Tristan in disguise), and so was able truthfully to swear to Mark that none but the king and the beggar had held her, so she was not burned when she took hold of the hot iron that was to prove to all who saw it that she had spoken the truth.

Tristan, however, had already hurried away from King Mark's court before Iseult's innocence could be proclaimed and had travelled to Duke Gilan in Swales,[4] who greeted him openly and made him feel welcome. Yet all the time he was there, Tristan could do nothing but think of Iseult. At this time, the land of Gilan was under the overlordship of a cruel giant named Urgan li vilus (literally Urgan the Vile), who allowed Gilan and his people to live free from molestation provided they pay him a tribute of sheep, cattle and pigs on an increasingly frequent basis.

Shortly after Tristan arrived, Urgan li vilus came to collect his tribute. Upon hearing how Gilan and his people were living under the threat of this giant, Tristan offered to rid Gilan of the troublesome ogre. Gilan offered Tristan anything within his power to give him in reward if he could do what no other had been able to do before. Tristan thus set forth and confronted Urgan li vilus just as he was about to drive off his tribute. Urgan li vilus killed Tristan's horse, but the knight replied by putting out one of the giant's eyes with his lance. Then, as the giant raced to where his own lance had fallen, Tristan cut off his right hand and then struck the giant's thigh a mighty blow. Now, for the first time ever, fearing for his life, Urgan li vilus picked up his hand and raced off to his home.

Tristan knew that he could not prove he had defeated Urgan li vilus, so he set off after the giant, following the trail of blood that had flowed from the wound in his thigh. Coming to the giant's fortress Tristan forced his way in, but could find no trace of the foul giant apart from his severed hand, which lay on the table, for the giant had gone in search of various herbs with which to heal his wounds, and also rejoin his hand to his arm. Tristan took the hand and returned to where he had first met the giant.

When Urgan li vilus came back and found that his hand had gone, he set off after Tristan and in his rage easily missed the knight when he sought to strike him dead. Tristan simply dodged the ragged swing of the giant's lance and put out the giant's other eye. Blindly Urgan li vilus swung his lance from left to right, but never once managed to hit Tristan, though if he had he would have killed the knight. Finally, Tristan managed to lead the giant towards a precipice and then charged him, so that he toppled over the edge and fell to his death.

Tristan recovered the severed hand from where he had hidden it and returned to Gilan, who kept his promise to give Tristan anything he desired. Tristan asked to be given Petitcrieu, the magical dog of Gilan that had been sent to him from the realms of Avalon. Petitcrieu is wonderfully described by Gottfried von Strassburg, who says that no one could accurately describe its colour, for:

> its breast it was so many-coloured that you would not have said otherwise than that it was whiter than snow; but at the loins it was greener than clover; one flank was redder than scarlet, the other yellower than saffron; underneath, it resembled azure, but above there was a mixture so finely blended that no one hue stood out from all the others – for here was neither green, nor red, nor white, nor black, nor yellow, nor blue, and yet a touch of them all, I mean a regular purple. If you looked at this rare work from Avalon against the grain of its coat, no one, however discerning, could have told you its colour. It was as bewilderingly varied as if there was no colour at all.

Though Gilan did not at first want to give up his most prized treasure, he was honour bound and handed the small animal over to Tristan who immediately wrote a letter to Iseult and had the dog sent to her at Tintagel. She received the gift from her maid who had met the messenger bringing the dog to her, and sent her back to him with a letter to Tristan telling him that it was safe for him to return as she had put Mark's mind at rest. Tristan, upon receiving her letter, immediately left Swales for Tintagel.

It was not long before the rumours about Tristan and Iseult started again, so once more Tristan took flight, this time crossing the English Channel and settling in Brittany. There he married the daughter of Hoe,[5] King of Brittany, who was known as Iseult of the White Hands. Various other names are given for Tristan's father-in-law: Havelin by Eilhart von Oberge in his twelfth-century *Tristant*; Jovelin, Duke of Arundel, by Gottfried von Strassburg in his masterly *Tristan and Isolde*; and Gilierchins in the fourteenth-century Italian *Tavola ritonda*. However, Tristan did not consummate his marriage with his wife, although he did become the firm friend of her brother Kahedrin. The latter fell in love with the Irish Iseult and wrote love letters to her. She replied in all innocence, but Tristan misunderstood and Kahedrin had to jump from a window to save being killed by the enraged Tristan, landing on a chess game that King Mark was playing below the window. Kahedrin eventually died of his love for Iseult.

Receiving yet another poisoned wound, Tristan believed that only Iseult, who had healed his earlier wound in Ireland, could again heal this one, and so sent for her to come to his aid. Before the ship departed to fetch Iseult, Tristan had obtained a promise from the captain that he would hoist white sails if Iseult were on board when he returned, but black sails if she had declined to come.[6] Jealous of her husband's undying love for Iseult, his wife lied to him on seeing the ship returning with white sails hoisted, saying instead that they were black. On hearing this Tristan died, and when Iseult arrived and found that Tristan was dead, she too died of a broken heart. King Mark buried them side by side, though Malory says that it was Mark who killed Tristan as he played the harp to Iseult by driving either a lance or a sword into his back. From Tristan's grave there grew a vine, while from Iseult's a rose sprang up. These two plants met and became inseparably entwined.

The origins of this famous love story are a little difficult to pin down. One suggestion is that it is Pictish, for Tristan is a Pictish name that would have originally been Drystan or Drostan, the *D* becoming a *T* seemingly to connect the name with the Latin *tristis*, which means 'sad'. This is further supported by Welsh tradition, which calls his father Tallwch, which is itself perhaps a form of the Pictish name Talorc. Welsh legend again supports this by saying that the lover of Esseyllt (the Welsh form of Iseult) is always Tristan son of Tallwch. Similarities in the story also suggest that the origin was none other than the story of Gráinne and Diarmaid ua Duibhne[7] from Irish mythology. The legend could possibly have been carried from Ireland to the Hiberno-Scottish kingdoms, and from these people to the Picts. Pictish king lists say that King Talorc III (ruled *c.*780), who was perhaps legendary, was succeeded by Drust V, leading to a possible identification between these two and the main characters of the legend. All these connections have generally led scholars to agree that Tristan was Drust, the son of King Talorc.

Obviously, there have been many modifications to the story as it became more widely known, and it is now almost universally accepted that the final version is Breton. However, there is a great deal that is uniquely Cornish.

Near Fowey in Cornwall there is a stone (unremarkably known as the Fowey Stone) that bears the earliest known inscription naming Tristan as the son of Cunomorus,[8] this inscription being thought to read *Drustans his iacit cunomori filius* – 'Here lies Tristan, son of Cunomorus.' Not far from Helston, Cornwall, in Meneage, is a ford that was recorded as Hryt Eselt in the tenth century – the earliest known form of Iseult. These two simple facts would seem to suggest that as the story passed through Cornwall, a local hero and heroine replaced those originally concerned with the story. King Mark himself is called King of Cornwall and is traditionally associated with Castle Dore near Galant. All these factors point directly to a Cornish origin, further supported in the earliest form of the romance itself, by the Norman-French poet Béroul. This firmly sets the story in south and mid-Cornwall, and mentions such places as Chapel Rock near Mevagissey (Tristan's Leap) and the Forest of Morrois (Moresk, near Truro), where the lovers once fled to hide from King Mark and his barons.

Other commentators have added more details to the story. Eilhart von Oberge says that Tristan (called Tristram by Sir Thomas Malory) was the first person to train dogs. Italian romance gave him and Iseult two children bearing their names, while the Icelandic *Saga of Tristram* says that Tristan had a son by Iseult of the White Hands who was named Kalegras. French romance give Tristan and Iseult a single son, Ysaie the Sad, and a grandson, Marc. Latterly the lovers became the subject of Richard Wagner's opera *Tristan and Isolde* that was first performed in 1865.

Sir Yvain

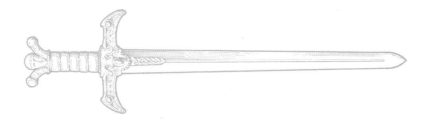

THE NAMING OF THIS KNIGHT is the responsibility of Chrétien de Troyes, as he was originally known as Owain, one of the Twenty-four Knights of King Arthur's Court, a historical character who was the son of Urien of Rheged, whom he succeeded. He has subsequently passed into the realms of myth and legend and has countless associations with Arthur. Although he certainly lived later than the traditional Arthurian period – he was said to have heavily defeated the British *c.*593 – both he and his father have been drawn into Arthurian legend. In this role he is the son of Urien by Arthur's sister Morgan Le Fay, who appears to have her origins in the goddess Modron,[1] whom some Welsh sources name as the mother of Owain. Welsh tradition made him the husband of Penarwan, who was unfaithful to him according to the *Trioedd Ynys Prydein*, and Denw, the daughter of Anna and Lot, and thus a niece of Arthur. The *Mabinogion* story of the *Dream of Rhonabwy* has Owain and Arthur playing *gwyddbwyll* – a type of board game – during which Owain's ravens fought with Arthur's men and were almost defeated. However, Owain raised his flag, and the ravens set about their opponents with renewed vigour. Sir Owain's traditional genealogy is as below:

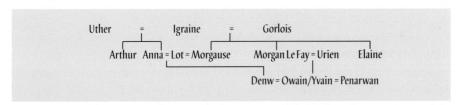

French romance gives us the most detail about the Arthurian Owain, particularly the French romance *Yvain*[2] by Chrétien de Troyes, which some consider to be his masterpiece. In this, Owain, who is called Yvain, learns of a wondrous spring or fountain in the Forest of Broceliande[3] from another knight, named by some as Sir Kymon or Sir Calogrenant and made the cousin of Yvain, who had been defeated by the knight that protected the spring. Sir Yvain was eager for adventure and so travelled to the forest. There, exactly as he had been told, he encountered the knight whose name was Esclados. He was dressed from head to foot in black – yet another occurrence of a Black Knight in the Arthurian cycle – and rode the most magnificent black stallion that Yvain had ever laid eyes on.

Yvain challenged the Black Knight, who had previously defeated all who dared to risk themselves against him. However, this time he had met his match. Not only did Yvain defeat him but he also inflicted a mortal wound on him. Esclados, realizing that he was done for, turned tail and rode as quickly as he could back towards his castle, with Yvain hot on his heels.

Soon they came to a magnificent castle that challenged even Camelot in its grandeur. Esclados rode swiftly across the drawbridge, the outer portcullis dropping as soon as he had passed, and tripped a hidden mechanism. However, Yvain was so close to the fleeing knight that the portcullis cut his own horse in half directly behind the saddle, leaving him trapped between the inner and outer gates to the castle. While he was pondering his position, a beautiful lady, Lunete, came to him and gave him a ring that had the power to make him invisible if he wore it with the stone reversed and clenched in his fist. She told him to evade the castle guards when they came for him by using the ring and she would hide him.

Yvain followed the instructions he had been given and soon found himself hidden away in the castle. That night a great wailing was heard as the women of the castle mourned the passing of Esclados who had just died. The following morning Yvain caught a glimpse of the mistress of the castle and was immediately smitten. She was the widow of Esclados, whose name was Laudine de Landuc, the daughter of Duke Laudunet and the sister of Lunete. Lunete agreed to woo her sister for Yvain, and finally persuaded her to marry the knight, for there could be no more suitable husband for her than the only knight who had ever been able to defeat Esclados.

After his marriage, which made him the lord of all Esclados's domains and protector of the fountain in the forest, Sir Yvain carried out his duties and fought off all who came to challenge him. Many of these he held for ransom, distributing the money among the needy of his realm. For three years Sir Yvain lived a life of happiness with Laudine.

As no news of Sir Yvain had been heard at Arthur's court for three years, the king, along with Sir Gawain, Sir Kay and Sir Kymon, set off for the Forest of Broceliande to determine what had happened to their comrade. There they encountered the Black Knight with the visor of his helmet down, neither party recognizing the other. First Yvain unseated Sir Kay and then he defeated Sir

Gawain, whose helmet flew off as he hit the ground. Yvain immediately dismounted, threw off his own helmet and rushed to the side of his fallen comrade, apologizing profusely for not having recognized him with his visor down. Having been reunited with his friends, Yvain led them back to his castle, introduced them to his wife and entertained them regally, Sir Gawain using the time to get very close to Lunete. The following morning Sir Yvain departed with King Arthur and his comrades, promising Laudine that he would be away for only three months.

However, once back at Camelot, Sir Yvain quickly forgot about Laudine and three months became three years. Then one day a noble lady appeared riding a magnificent horse. She found Yvain and, scolding him, removed the ring from his finger that he had worn since Lunete had first given it to him. Immediately Yvain remembered Laudine and, overcome with shame and grief, fled from the court and took to living like an animal in the woods and forests.

Having lived for some time in the open, foraging for whatever food he could find, and close to death from starvation and exposure, Sir Yvain was found by a widowed lady and her handmaidens. They restored Yvain to full health with the use of magical potions and ointments and then, although they begged him to remain with them, armed him and bade him farewell. Shortly afterwards Yvain came across a foul serpent in battle with a lion. Yvain killed the serpent, after which the lion would not leave his side, thus earning him the nickname the Knight of the Lion. The lion caught food for Yvain and watched over him as he slept at night.

For many months Yvain and the lion led a solitary life, until one day Yvain heard the sighs of a maiden in distress and, although he could not see her, questioned her, only to discover that it was none other than Lunete, who had been condemned to death for not having brought Yvain back with her to her sister Laudine. Yvain waited patiently until he saw Lunete being led to the place of her execution by two knights, whom he and the lion defeated, and thus rescued Lunete. Together they rode back to the castle of Laudine, and there Yvain was reconciled with his wife. A short time later Yvain, Laudine and Lunete travelled to Camelot, where they would remain until they died.

The final episode of Yvain's life concerns his defeat of a huge black giant whom he overcame, again with the assistance of the lion, releasing 24 maidens who were the giant's prisoners. So impressed by the prowess of Yvain and the lion was the giant that he promised to give up his evil ways and keep a hospice for travellers for as long as he should live.

Authors and Sources

It should be noted that those works listed here, and the authors briefly detailed, are by no means *all* the sources of the Arthurian legends, but are simply those that have been referred to during the compilation of this book.

Afollonau

'Appletrees', a Welsh Myrddin (Merlin) poem that names Chwimleian as a flower maiden. The title is interesting as it was believed in folk-lore that to rest beneath an apple tree would leave you at the mercy of the fairies. An excellent translation of this poem is to be found in *Merlin Through the Ages* by R.J. Stewart and John Matthews (Blandford, London, 1995).

Alliterative Morte Arthure

Anonymous 4,346 line Middle English poem dating from c.1400 that tells of Arthur's war against Rome and the Romans, the rebellion of Mordred and Arthur's final battle. The poem is notable for including the Amazons of classical Greek mythology, saying that they were the subjects of the Roman Emperor Lucius Hiberius.

Aneurin

Welsh court poet who flourished in the late sixth and early seventh centuries and is the alleged author of *The Gododdin*. Aneurin is usually made a contemporary of Taliesin and, like that famous bard, had courtly connections with King Urien of Rheged.

Annales Cambriae

Anonymous set of Welsh annals that date from the tenth century, though based on much earlier material. Notoriously unreliable for the dating methods used, the *Annales Cambriae* mention the battles of Badon and Camlann, saying that both Mordred and Arthur fell in the latter, without saying that they were on opposing sides.

Annales Toledanos

Anonymous Spanish annals that say that the battle of Camlann was fought in 580, the latest recorded date for the last battle of Arthur's reign.

Annals of Tigernach
Anonymous Irish annals that date the battle of Camlann as 541.

Ariosto, Ludovico
Italian poet (1474–1533), born in Reggio nell'Emilia. Originally intending to train for a career in law, he abandoned that in favour of poetry. In 1503 he entered court of the Cardinal Ippolito d'Este at Ferrara and over ten years produced *Orlando Furioso* (1516), the Roland epic that forms a continuation of Boiardo's *Orlando Innamorato*. Over the next sixteen years he revised and expanded his *Orlando Furioso* until, in 1532, it was published as a third edition, the form it exists in today. He died the following year and was buried in the church of San Benedetto at Ferrara, where a magnificent monument marks the last resting place of this great Italian romancer.

Armes Prydein
'The Prophecy of Britain', a heroic tenth century Welsh poem that was probably written between 900 and 930. It remains unique as being the first work to refer to the magician Myrddin (Merlin). The poem calls upon the British to unite against the Saxon invaders and foretells that the last British king, Cadwalladr, will rise again to lead a great army, including the Men of Dublin, the Irish Gaels, the Men of Cornwall and the Men of Strathclyde, which will drive the Saxons back into the sea. The resurrection of Cadwalladr in this poem may have given rise to the concept that Arthur would one day return from Avalon.

Bede, The Venerable
Anglo-Saxon scholar, theologian and historian (*c*.673–735) who was born near Monkwearmouth, Durham. He was placed into the care of Benedict Biscop at the age of seven at the monastery of Wearmouth, and in 682 moved to the new monastery of Jarrow, Northumberland. He was ordained there in 703 and remained a monk for the rest of his life. A prolific writer, Bede produced homilies, lives of saints, lives of abbots, hymns, epigrams, works on chronology, grammar and the physical sciences, as well as commentaries on the Old and New Testaments. His greatest work was his *Historia Ecclesiastica Gentis Anglorum* ('Ecclesiastical History of the English People') which he completed in 731. It remains the single most important source for early English history.

Béroul
Twelfth-century French writer about whom very little can be said for certain. He was the author of an Anglo-Norman *Tristan* romance.

Boece, Hector
Scottish historian (*c*.1465–1536) born in Dundee. He studied at Montaigu College, Paris, where from c.1492 to 1498 he was regent, or professor of philosophy. Invited to preside over the new university of Aberdeen, Boece accepted the position and was at the same time made a canon of the cathedral. In 1522 he published, in Latin, his lives of the bishops of Mortlach and Aberdeen. His *Scotorum Historia* (History of Scotland) contains Arthurian material written from an anti-Arthur viewpoint. Published in 1527, this work was deemed distinctly critical at the time, though it subsequently proved to contain much that was fictional.

Boiardo, Matteo Maria

Italian poet (1434–94), born in Scandiano at the foot of the Lombard Apennines. He studied at Ferrara and in 1462 married the daughter of the Count of Norellara. He lived at the court of Ferrara and was appointed governor of Modena in 1481 and of Reggio in 1487. His fame rests on his unfinished *Orlando Innamorato* (1486), a long narrative piece in which the Charlemagne romances are recast in *ottava rima* (Italian stanza of eight 11-syllabled lines – ten-syllabled in English – the first six lines rhyming alternatively, the last two forming a couplet). This poem was to inspire the *Orlando Furioso* of Ariosto.

Boun, Rauf de

French chronicler and author of the *Petit Brut* about whose life nothing is known.

Breta Sogur

Scandinavian version of the works of Geoffrey of Monmouth that names Assysla as the island to which the dying Arthur was taken. The work is also unique in asserting that Arthur was buried at Canterbury, a concept that appears nowhere else.

Brut

Thought to have been written between c.1189 and c.1199 by Layamon, this Anglo-Saxon alliterative verse chronicle, a history of England which contains a great deal of Arthurian material, is a translation from French and an amplification of the slightly earlier *Roman de Brut* by Robert Wace. The work is especially important in the history of English versification as the first poem written in Middle English.

Carl of Carlisle, The

Incomplete sixteenth-century English romance that is based on the earlier fourteenth century *Sir Gawain and the Carl of Carlisle*, which is also unfinished. The work possibly just echoes the earlier one by also remaining incomplete.

Chevalier de la charette, Le

French romance written by Chrétien de Troyes c.1170 that introduces the character of Sir Lancelot. Chrétien de Troyes says that the story of the love affair between Lancelot and Guinevere was given to him by his patroness, Marie de Champagne, which may certainly be the case, for the story of an illicit love affair between a knight and a queen is known to have pre-existed the text of Chrétien de Troyes.

Childe Rowland

Medieval Scottish ballad that tells of how Ellen, Arthur's daughter, was saved from an enchanted, Otherworldly, prison by her brother, hence Arthur's son, Rowland.

Chrétien de Troyes

Medieval French poet and troubadour who was born in Troyes, in Champagne, some time during the middle of the twelfth century. The greatest of the medieval French poets, Chrétien de Troyes was the author of the earliest romances dealing with King Arthur. A member of the court of the Countess Marie de Champagne, daughter of King Louis VII, he dedicated his metrical romance of courtly love *Yvain et Lancelot* to his patroness. He is best known simply for the number of Arthurian romances he wrote: *Erec et Enide* (c.1160); *Le chevalier de la charette*, which is also simply known as *Lancelot*; *Cligés* (c.1164); *Le chevalier au lion*, also called *Yvain*; and *Le conte de graal*, also called *Perceval* (c.1180), which he wrote for Philip, Count of Flanders, but which remained unfinished at the time of his death in 1183. His works are reputed to be the first to introduce the concept of the Holy Grail and are essential to any study of the Arthurian cycle.

Cligés

Written c.1164 by Chrétien de Troyes, this romance concerns the exploits of Cligés, the son of Alexander, Emperor of Constantinople, and Soredamor, the daughter of Lot. While his uncle Alis was emperor he married Fenice, with whom Cligés fell in love. Unable to make his feelings known, he travelled to the court of King Arthur and became a Knight of the Round Table. After Alis had died, he returned to Constantinople and duly married Fenice.

Conte de graal, Le

Unfinished pre-thirteenth-century work by Chrétien de Troyes, the 484-line prologue to the work being known as the *Elucidation*. This poem is considered the earliest work that enhances the legends of King Arthur and introduces the concept of the Holy Grail. Its incomplete state gave rise to a series of *Continuations*, the first of these appearing *c.*1200.

Continuations

Name given to a number of works that appeared after the death of Chrétien de Troyes in 1183 that attempted to complete *Le conte de graal*. The first appeared *c.*1200, the second some time during the thirteenth century, while Gerbert and Manessier also produced *Continuations* during the same century.

Culhwch and Olwen

Complex and possibly incomplete pre-eleventh-century romance that forms a part of the *Mabinogion*. It tells the story of Culhwch, Arthur's cousin, and his quest to locate and win the hand of Olwen, the daughter of the chief giant of Wales, Yspaddaden. This section of the *Mabinogion* forms perhaps the most important part for the Arthurian student, as within its complex structure many of the characters who were later developed into the leading lights of the Arthurian cycle can be found in possibly their original form.

de Boron, Robert

Burgundian author (*fl.* 1200) or two very important Arthurian romances, about whose life very little is known. His works were *Joseph d'Arimathia*, which deals with the Grail legends, and *Merlin*. It is thought that he may also have been responsible for the *Didot Perceval*.

De Excidio et Conquestu Britanniae

A famous treatise that was probably written between 516 and 547 by the British writer Gildas, thus making it contemporary with the traditional Arthurian period. This work, which is the only contemporary extant history of the Celts, mentions the battle of Badon, but does not name King Arthur.

Didot Perceval

French prose romance dating from *c.*1200 that tells of Sir Perceval's quest for the Holy Grail. Even though the author of this work remains unknown, it has been suggested that he may have been Robert de Boron.

Diu Crône

Thirteenth-century romance by Heinrich von dem Türlin in which Sir Gawain features as the hero who achieves the quest for the Holy Grail.

Dryden, John

English poet (1631–1700) whose opera *King Arthur*, with music by Henry Purcell, has little true Arthurian content, for in it Arthur is in love with a blind girl by the name of Emmeline, who is also loved by Arthur's enemy, Oswald, a Saxon king.

Eilhart von Oberge
Twelfth-century German author of *Tristant* which gives just one of the many versions of the tragic love story of Tristan and Iseult.

Elucidation
The name by which the 484-line prologue to *Le conte de graal* by Chrétien de Troyes is known.

Enfaces Gauvain
Thirteenth-century French poem concerning the life of Sir Gawain which is unusual in that it makes Lot, Gawain's father by Morgause, a page at Arthur's court.

Estoire del Sainte Graal
Thirteenth-century French romance that forms a part of the *Vulgate Version*. It remains unique for associating the Waste Land of the Grail legends with Wales, an association found nowhere else.

Faerie Queene, The
Epic, unfinished, allegorical work by Edmund Spenser that features the youthful, uncrowned King Arthur and remains that poet's most famous work. In the poem England is represented as Fairyland, where in which Arthur had adventures before becoming king, and where he became enamoured of Gloriana, Spenser's representation of Queen Elizabeth I.

Geoffrey of Monmouth
Twelfth-century Welsh author (*c.*1100–*c.*1154) of two highly important Arthurian works in Latin. Thought to be the son of Breton parents, Geoffrey studied at Oxford from *c.*1129, when he signed his name to the foundation charter of Oseney Abbey, and was Archdeacon of Llandarff or Monmouth (*c.*1140), being appointed bishop of St Asaph, north Wales, in 1152. In 1153 he witnessed the Treaty of Winchester between King Stephen and Henry of Anjou. Welsh records say that he died in 1155. His totally fictitious *Historia Regum Britanniae* (*History of the Kings of England*) deals with a pseudo-mythical history of Britain that was, according to him, based on an earlier Welsh or British work that he alone had seen and which had been given to his friend Walter, the Archdeacon of Oxford. Though worthless as history, the book features a substantial Arthurian section and was the first work to give a coherent narrative of the life of King Arthur as known today. His second work, the *Vita Merlini* (*Life of Merlin*) is a poetic description of Merlin's adventures and his madness.

Gest of Sir Gauvain
Thirteenth-century English verse romance that includes details of the combat between Sir Gawain and Brandiles, but today survives only in a fragmentary condition.

Gildas, Saint
Romano-British historian and monk working in the traditional Arthurian period. Born in Strathclyde, he fled the strife that raged in his neighbourhood and went to Wales where he married, becoming a monk only after his wife had died. His famous *De Excidio et Conquestu Britanniae* was probably written between 516 and 547, while Gildas was still quite a young man. Though it does not mention Arthur by name, it does mentions the battle of Badon, and is the only contemporary history of the Celts, giving the British version of events from the

Roman invasion to his own time. Gildas was revered by later writers, for in the *Mabinogion* he appears as Arthur's counsellor, which might be a historical fact.

Giraldus Cambrensis

Norman-Welsh chronicler and ecclesiastic (*c.*1146–*c.*1223) of noble parents who was born in Manorbier Castle, Dyfed. He was educated at the abbey of St Peter, Gloucester, and later studied in Paris. He became archdeacon of St David's, but when his uncle, the bishop, died in 1176, he was overlooked for the position as he was a Welshman. After he was again overlooked for the vacancy in 1198, he concentrated on his studies and his writing. Though by no means a major Arthurian source, he did comment on Merlin's madness, but also said that there were two Merlins, one a wizard and the other a wild man.

Gododdin, The

Traditionally ascribed to the Welsh court poet Aneurin who flourished in the late sixth and early seventh centuries, this poem, which celebrates the British heroes from Gododdin, a realm which stretched from the Forth to the Tees, who were annihilated by the Saxons *c.*600 in Yorkshire, can claim to contain the first literary allusion to Arthur, though the relevant line is thought by some to be a later addition.

Gottfried von Strassburg

Thirteenth-century author (*fl.* 1200) of the masterly German romance *Tristan and Isolde*, which was based on the earlier work by the Anglo-Norman poet Thomas. Little or nothing is known about his life, but he was famous as an early exponent of literary criticism, having left appraisals of the poets of the period. Later writers referred to him

as a *meister*, which implies that he had a university education.

Green Knight, The

Based on the earlier *Sir Gawain and the Green Knight*, this version, which dates from *c.*1500, is an inferior telling of the famous incident between Sir Gawain and the Green Knight.

Hartmann von Aue

Twelfth-century (*c.*1170–1215) German poet of the Middle High German period as well as a participant in the Crusade of 1197. His two Arthurian works, *Iwain* and *Erec*, closely follow the works of Chrétien de Troyes.

Heinrich von dem Türtin

Thirteenth-century poet from Germany and the author of the *Diu Crône*. Almost nothing is known about his life.

Heywood, Thomas

Seventeenth-century author (*c.*1574–1641) author of the *Life of Merlin*. Born in Lincolnshire, the son of a clergyman, he was educated at Cambridge and was known to be writing plays by 1596. Up to 1633 he had a hand in the composition of 220 plays, though today only 24 of his plays have survived.

Historia Britonum

Clumsily put together Latin work that is traditionally ascribed to Nennius and perhaps dates from the ninth century. The work purports to give an account of British history from the time of Julius Caesar to towards the end of the seventh century. It gives a mythical account of the origins of the British people and recounts the Roman occupation, the settlement of the Saxons and King Arthur's 12 victories. Although it contains fanciful material of doubtful historicity, its real value lies in its preservation of material needed for the study of early Celtic literature in general, and the Arthurian legends in particular.

Historia Regum Britanniae

History of the Kings of Britain, the pseudo-mythical, eleventh-century Latin account by Geoffrey of Monmouth of the early kings of Britain, contains a substantial Arthurian section and gives the first coherent narrative of the legends surrounding King Arthur as they are known today.

Iwain

Middle High German romance by the twelfth-century poet Hartmann von Aue that clearly follows the earlier works of Chrétien de Troyes. The hero of the romance, Iwain, is usually known as Owain or Yvain.

Joseph d'Arimathia

Twelfth-century work by the Burgundian Robert de Boron that deals with the Grail legends, especially those surrounding the biblical associations of Jesus's uncle Joseph of Arimathea.

King Arthur

Opera written in 1691 by John Dryden, with music by Henry Purcell, that has little or no true Arthurian content, for in it Arthur is in love with the blind Emmeline, who is also loved by the Saxon Oswald, Arthur's enemy.

Lady of Shalott, The

Famous poem by Alfred, Lord Tennyson that tells the story of Elaine, the daughter of Bernard of Astolat, who falls in love with Sir Lancelot and then dies of her unrequited passion for the knight.

Layamon

A Worcestershire poet and priest at Ernley (now Areley Regis) on the Severn near Bewdley. In *c.*1200 he wrote an alliterative verse chronicle, the Anglo-Saxon *Brut*, a history of England, which contains much Arthurian material and was an amplification of Robert Wace's slightly earlier *Roman de Brut*. It is an important work in the history of English versification as the first poem written in Middle English.

Lestoire de Merlin

That part of the *Vulgate Version* giving one version of the life of Merlin.

Livre d'Artus

A French continuation to *Merlin* by Robert de Boron.

Lybius Desconus

Fourteenth-century English poem concerning the adventures of the eponymous hero whose name means 'The Fair Unknown One'. Also known as Le Bel Inconnu, this character was actually Guinglain, the illegitimate son of Gawain, who was raised in ignorance of his true ancestry. His nickname was given to him by the ever impertinent Sir Kay.

Mabinogion

A major Welsh source whose title is taken from *mabinogi* – 'instruction for young poets'. It is of prime importance to the Arthurian student. Drawn from *The White Book of Rhydderch* (1300–25) and *The Red Book of Hergest* (1375–1425), the *Mabinogion* was compiled in the mid-nineteenth century and is a collection of medieval Welsh myths and folk tales. Properly speaking, the *Mabinogion* consists of four tales: *Pwyll, Branwen ferch Llyr* (*Branwen, daughter of Llyr*), *Manawydan fab Llyr* (*Manawydan, son of Llyr*) and *Math fab*

Mathonwy (*Math, son of Mathonwy*), three of which concern the character of Pryderi, but none of which are Arthurian. By extension, the *Mabinogion* has come to include the Arthurian stories of *Gereint and Enid*, *Culhwch and Olwen*, *Owain*, *Peredur* and *Dream of Rhonabwy*. Possibly the most famous translation of all, that by Lady Charlotte Guest, also includes the story of *Taliesin*.

Malmesbury, William of

English chronicler (*c.*1090–*c.*1143), born probably near Malmesbury, Wiltshire. He became a monk in the monastery at Malmesbury, and in due time became librarian and precentor. He took part in the council at Winchester in 1141 against King Stephen. His *Gesta Regum Anglorum* provides a lively history of the kings of England from the Saxon invasion to 1126. The *Historia Novella* brings the narrative down to 1142. His *Gesta Pontificum* is an ecclesiastical history of the bishops and chief monasteries of England to 1123. Other works of his include an account of the church at Glastonbury and lives of St Dunstan and St Wulfstan.

Malory, Sir Thomas

A fifteenth-century knight about whose life very little can be said with any certainty. He is most famous as the author of *Le Morte d'Arthur*, which was printed by Caxton in 1485 and is for many the classic Arthuriad. Caxton's preface to this work states that Malory was a knight, that he finished the work in the ninth year of the reign of King Edward IV (*c.*1470) and that he 'reduced' it from a French book. It is now thought that he was the Sir Thomas Malory of Newbold Revel, Warwickshire, whose quarrels with a neighbouring priory and (probably) Lancastrian politics resulted in his imprisonment, although many cannot believe that the author of the greatest masterpiece of English Arthurian romance could possibly have been a violent criminal. Following the death of his father, John, in 1433, Thomas and his brother-in-law, Eustace Burnaby, were charged with an armed robbery in Northamptonshire. In 1445 he was elected Member of Parliament for Warwickshire and married Elizabeth Walsh. In 1450 he became the Member of Parliament for Wareham in Dorset, having been put forward by the Duke of York. Malory was violently opposed to his patron's enemy, the Duke of Buckingham. As a result he was accused of attempting to ambush the Duke on 4 January 1450 with 36 men. He was acquitted, but further charges of theft, rape and extortion were brought against him. Again he was acquitted. The following year, however, he was imprisoned in July 1451 for deer poaching and cattle rustling from the Duke of Buckingham's estate at Caludon in Wiltshire. He escaped and broke into Combe Abbey twice in two days, stealing a large number of treasures. He was soon recaptured and spent the best part of the next ten years in prison. Released on bail for a brief spell in 1454, Malory committed another robbery in Essex and was quickly thrown back into gaol. In 1462 a general pardon was issued by the new Yorkist monarch King Edward IV. At this point Malory was definitely a Yorkist. However, in 1468 he was specifically named as one of 15 who were excluded from another general pardon, for he had apparently switched allegiance. It was during this, his final period in prison, that he was to write his masterpiece. Of Caxton's black-letter folio, only two copies now exist. An independent manuscript was discovered at Winchester in 1934. *Le Morte d'Arthur* is the best prose romance in English and was a happy attempt to give epic unity to the whole mass of French Arthurian literature.

Marie de France

Twelfth-century (*fl. c.*1160–90) French poet and author of two Arthurian romances, *Chevrefueil* and *Lanval*. Born in Normandy, she spent most of her life in England where she wrote her *Lais* sometime before 1167 and her *Fables* some time after 1170. She translated into French the *Tractatus de Purgatorio Sancti Patricii* (*c.*1190) and her works contain many classical allusions. The *Lais*, her most important work, comprises fourteen romantic narratives in octosyllabic verse based on Celtic material.

Merlin

Important twelfth-century romance concerning the life and exploits of Merlin that was written by the Burgundian author Robert de Boron.

Merveilles de Rigomer

More commonly referred to simply as *Rigomer*, this thirteenth-century verse romance tells the story of the adventures of Sir Gawain and Sir Lancelot. It was allegedly written by an obscure poet named Jehan, about whom nothing is known.

Mort Artu

Fully titled *Le Mort le Roi Artu*, this French romance, possibly one of the finest examples of medieval French romantic writing, forms the final section of the *Vulgate Version*. It was written *c.*1230–35 by someone who was familiar with the other sections of the *Vulgate Version*, though he did not write them himself.

Morte Arthure

Middle English poem by Thomas Heywood (*c.*1574–1641) that was written towards the end of the sixteenth century in rhyming stanzas and is a vigorous adaptation of the French tale on which it is based.

Morte d'Arthur, Le

Completed in 1470 and published by Caxton in 1485 as one of the first books to use modern printing techniques, this fifteenth-century work by Sir Thomas Malory comprises a series of episodes from the life of King Arthur. It is regarded as the first great prose work in English literature, but in actual fact only the last eight books of the series are entitled *Le Morte d'Arthur*. The series omits a few of the tales and contains many inconsistencies, particularly in its multitude of Elaines and wounded kings. However, it still remains the main English source of the Arthurian legends and is an undoubted literary masterpiece.

Nennius

Welsh writer (*fl.* 769) who was reputedly the author of the clumsily put together Latin work *Historia Britonum*, which purports to give a history of Britain from the time of Julius Caesar until the end of the seventh century.

Orlando Furioso

Italian Carolingian romance by Ludovico Ariosto that forms a sequel to the unfinished *Orlando Innamorato* of Matteo Maria Boiardo. It was published in its final form in 1532. Featuring some Arthurian material, the poem describes the unrequited love of Orlando for Angelica, set against the war between the Saracens and the Christians during Charlemagne's reign. It influenced Shakespeare, Milton and Byron, and is considered to be the perfect poetic expression of the Italian Renaissance.

Orlando Innamorato

Unfinished epic narrative poem of 1486, written by Matteo Maria Boiardo, in which the Charlemagne romances were recast in *ottava rima*. The work gave rise to the *Orlando Furioso* of Ariosto.

Owain

Welsh prose romance from the thirteenth century that is to be found in the *Mabinogion*, and concerning the exploits of Owain the son of Urien of Rheged.

Pa gur

Famous Welsh poem that tells how Sir Kay travelled to Anglesey with a view to killing lions, especially preparing himself for an encounter with a monstrous feline animal known as the Cath Palug.

Parsifal

Thirteenth-century work by Wolfram von Eschenbach that recounts a Teutonic version of the Arthurian legends, especially those concerning Sir Perceval. In later times this work influenced the composer Richard Wagner, who based his opera *Parsifal* on it. The opera was first performed in 1882, just one year before the sudden death of the composer.

Pedwar Marchog ar Hugan Llys Arthur

Important fifteenth-century, if not earlier, Welsh work which gives a list of knights at Arthur's court. These knights, thought to represent a company founded before the Knights of the Round Table, were referred to as the Twenty-four Knights of King Arthur's Court.

Perceval

Work by Chrétien de Troyes that is probably better known as *Le conte de graal*. Written for Philip, Count of Flanders, and started *c.*1180, it remained unfinished due to the author's death *c.*1183. Several *Continuations* subsequently appeared, each attempting to finish what Chrétien had started.

Peredur

Welsh romance concerning the exploits of the eponymous hero (later to become Sir Perceval) that became a part of the *Mabinogion*.

Perlesvaus

A thirteenth-century French prose romance concerning the quest for the Holy Grail.

Preiddeu Annwfn

Spoils of Annwfn, an early Welsh poem dating from *c.*900, allegedly written by the great Taliesin. It describes an expedition Arthur led to the Otherworld to obtain an enchanted cauldron. It details various aspects of the supernatural realm, which was organized, so it would seem, along the same lines as Hades, the classical Greek land of the dead. It is thought that this poem was one of the origins of the later Grail legends.

Prophécies de Merlin

Thirteenth-century French work detailing the life and prophecies of Merlin. It was allegedly written by Richard of Ireland.

Prose Lancelot

Thirteenth-century French prose romance that forms a part of the *Vulgate Version*.

Prose Merlin

Name given to two medieval romances about Merlin, one French and one English.

Prose Tristan

Thirteenth-century French work that describes, at length, the career of Tristan.

Queste del Sainte Graal

Thirteenth-century French romance that forms a part of the *Vulgate Version*. It describes the quest for the Holy Grail and introduces Sir Galahad as the knight who was pure enough to achieve the object of the quest. It is thought to have been written by a Cistercian because of its style and content.

Red Book of Hergest, The

Fourteenth-century manuscript that, along with *The White Book of Rhydderch*, contains the *Mabinogion* cycle.

Roman de Brut

Written in French in the twelfth century by Robert Wace, this work contains the first literary reference to the Round Table. It was quickly translated and expanded by Layamon in his *Brut*, which was written between 1189 and 1199.

Saga of Tristram

The title of two renditions of the legend of Tristan and Iseult. One is Norwegian and dates from 1266 and the other, which is undated is Icelandic. They are generally confused with each other and are more commonly known simply as *Tristram's Saga*.

Saga of Tristan and Isodd

Icelandic version of the story of Tristan and Iseult, which names Tristan's mother as Kalegras.

Scotorum Historia

Written by the Scottish historian Hector Boece, this work is interesting in that it contains Arthurian material written from an anti-Arthur viewpoint.

Sir Gawain and the Carl of Carlisle

Unfinished English romance that dates from *c.*1400 and relates the tale of Sir Gawain and his dealings with the Carl of Carlisle. It was later followed in the sixteenth century by a new version, *Carl of Carlisle*, that was again unfinished, though this may have been a deliberate ploy.

Sir Gawain and the Green Knight

One of the most famous of pieces of Arthurian literature, this anonymous English poem, which survives only as a single manuscript, together with three other poems by the same poet, dates from *c.*1346 and deals with the beheading contest entered into by Sir Gawain. It was followed approximately 100 years later by the much inferior *The Green Knight*.

Sir Perceval of Galles

Fourteenth-century English romance that tells the story of Sir Perceval but makes no mention of the Holy Grail or his part in the quest for that Holy vessel.

Spenser, Edmund

English poet (*c.*1552–99) who, though not much read in modern times, was regarded as the Virgil of his day, enjoying great popularity among his peers. His most famous work was the epic, unfinished, allegorical *Faerie Queene*, which features the uncrowned King Arthur.

Stanzaic Morte Arthur

3,969-line English poem that possibly dates from the fourteenth century and deals with the latter part of Arthur's life.

Tavola ritonda

Invaluable Italian source that dates from the fourteenth century and deals with a considerable number of Arthurian stories.

Thomas

Anglo-Norman poet who flourished in the twelfth century and was the author of Tristan, the earliest extant text, dating from 1155–70, of the legend of Tristan and Iseult. A fragment of 3,144 lines covering the final episodes of the story, including the deaths of the lovers, still survives.

Trioedd Ynys Prydein

Commonly referred to as the *Triads*, the collective name given to three collections of Welsh verse listing items in groups of three. Each contains a great deal of Arthurian material, but while two sets are considered genuine, the third has been the subject of intense controversy and is now considered a later emulation.

Tristan

Twelfth-century text by the Anglo-Norman poet Thomas that survives in a fragment of 3,144 lines. It is the earliest extant text covering the tragic love affair, written between *c.*1155 and *c.*1170. The fragment covers the final episodes of the story, including the deaths of the ill-fated lovers.

Tristan and Isolde

Early thirteenth-century (*c.*1210) Middle High German courtly epic by Gottfried von Strassburg, which was based on the earlier version of the story by the Anglo-Norman poet Thomas.

Turk and Gawain

English poem thought to date from the very end of the fifteenth century that tells the story of Gromer, who, through an enchantment, had been transformed into a Turk, resuming his normal form again only after Sir Gawain had, at his own request, cut off Gromer's head.

Ulrich von Zarzikhoven

Swiss or German author (*fl.* 1200) of *Lanzelet*, which differs quite markedly from the story of Lancelot as told by Chrétien de Troyes and other romancers.

Vita Merlini

Life of Merlin, an important Latin poetic description of the adventures of Merlin and his madness. It dates from the twelfth century and was written by Geoffrey of Monmouth some time after his *Historia Regum Britanniae.*

Vulgate Version

Thirteenth-century French collection of prose romances that consists of the *Prose Lancelot*; the *Queste del Sainte Graal* and its prelude, *Estoire del Sainte Graal*; the *Mort Artu*; the *Vulgate Merlin* and the *Vulgate Merlin Continuation.*

Wace, Robert

Twelfth-century author (*c.*1115–83), born in Jersey. His *Roman de Brut* contains a substantial Arthurian section and is most notable for making the first literary reference to the Round Table. It is a free Norman-French version of Geoffrey of Monmouth's *Historia Regum Britanniae*. Wace also wrote a number of other works, most notably the *Roman de Rou*, an epic account of the exploits of the Dukes of Normandy.

White Book of Rhydderch, The

Fourteenth-century manuscript that, along with The *Red Book of Hergest*, contains the *Mabinogion* cycle. It is today housed in the National Library of Wales, Aberystwyth, along with The *Black Book of Carmarthen* and The *Book of Taliesin*.

Wolfram von Eschenbach
German poet (*fl.* 1200) and author of *Parsifal,* a work that dealt with the Grail quest and Sir Perceval's part in it. He claimed that his source was the writer Kyot, but the existence of Kyot has been seriously questioned. Wolfram is also remembered as the author of several other works.

Notes

Who Were the Celts?

1 Hyperborean is derived from two Greek words: *hyper* meaning 'beyond', and *Boreas*, the name of the north wind. The Hyperboreans were therefore the people who lived beyond the north wind.

2 *Fragmenta Historia Graecae*.

3 The Goidelic variant of the Celtic language differs from the Brythonic in that, where Brythonic has a 'p' sound (as in Old Welsh *map*), Goidelic has a 'q' sound (as in Gaelic *mac*).

4 *Leabhar Gabhála Éireann*, which is commonly known as *The Book of Invasions*. This twelfth-century pseudo-history lists six successive invasionary forces that landed and settled in Ireland, the last of which were the Goidelic Celts.

5 Carthage was an ancient Phoenician port in North Africa, approximately 16 kilometres (10 miles) north of modern Tunis. An immensely successful culture, Carthage once dominated most of the Mediterranean, but from the sixth century BC it was in conflict with Greece and finally fell to the Romans in 146 BC at the end of the third Punic War.

6 Phocis was a region of ancient Greece that included the city of Delphi.

The Celtic Invasion of Britain

1 Megalithic is derived from two Greek words: *mega*, meaning 'great', and *lithos*, meaning 'a stone'.

2 The Arthurian legends paid no attention to fact and made Merlin the magical builder of Stonehenge, saying that he transported the ring by magic from Ireland, where it had been erected by giants who had originally come from Africa.

The Roman Invasion

1 The same year that the Romans mercilessly slaughtered the Druids and their families on Anglesey.

2 Goddess of wisdom and consort of the sun. The Romans assimilated her with their own goddess Minerva to form the Romano-Celtic deity Sulis Minerva.

The Anglo-Saxon Invasions

1 There are six possible sites for this battle based on place-names alone. The most likely are Badbury Hill in Devon, Badbury Rings in Dorset or a hill near Bath. The sixth-century monk Gildas (*c*.490–573) records in his *De Excidio et Conquestu Britanniae*, the only extant history of the Celts between the time of the Roman invasion and his own time, the battle of Mount Badon, but regrettably does not mention who led the Celtic forces.

The Birth of Arthur

1 The *Annales Cambriae* name King Arthur as having fought at the battle of Badon in the following paragraph: 'Year 72 The battle of Badon in which Arthur bore the cross of our Lord Jesus Christ on his shoulders for three days and three nights, and the Britons were victors.' The dating of the year simply as 72 has led to untold confusion, and regrettably there is now no way of actually deciphering the year in question. The battle has, therefore, been placed anywhere between 490 and 540.
2 Catterick, Yorkshire.
3 Covering roughly the area of modern Cumbria.

The Quest for the Holy Grail

1 *Spoils of Annwfn*, an early Welsh poem that dates from *c*.900 and supposedly composed by the legendary bard Taliesin.
2 Complex and possibly incomplete pre-eleventh-century romance that today forms a part of the *Mabinogion*.

The Knights of the Round Table

1 The kingdom of Gore lay on the borders of Scotland, from which it was separated by the River Temper, which could be crossed only by two bridges, one like the edge of a sword and the other under water. If one of Arthur's knights entered Gore, then only Sir Lancelot could rescue him.
2 Apparently there were several Ladies of the Lake, for even though the one who presented King Arthur with Excalibur was killed by Sir Balin, there was another to whom Excalibur was returned after the battle of Camlann. Yet another appears as the lover of Merlin, and another as the foster mother of Sir Lancelot. Finally, there are those fairies who collect the dying king in their barge and carry him off to Avalon.
3 The father of Sir Lancelot and Sir Ector de Maris.
4 Scandinavia, though its use in the legends may signify an Otherworldly realm.
5 King of Ireland and father of the maiden Iseult, of whom more is told in the profile for Sir Tristan (see pages 149–54). Anguish may be the historical King Oenghus of Cashel in southern Ireland, who was believed to have reigned during the traditional Arthurian period.
6 *Gest of Sir Gauvain*, a thirteenth-century English verse romance.
7 The second *Continuation* to Chrétien de Troyes's *Perceval*.
8 King of Cornwall and the husband of Iseult. His story is inexorably linked with the legends of Tristan and Iseult (see profile for Sir Tristan, pages 149–54).
9 *Ymddiddan Arthur a'r Eryr*. The eagle was a bird of special significance to the Celts as it was believed to be the incarnation of the soul of a god. Later this tradition made the bird the reincarnation of the soul of a saint.
10 King of Lothian, Orkney and Norway and brother-in-law of King Arthur. His

name appears to simply mean 'Lothian ruler'.

11 A kingdom separated from Arthur's kingdom by the River Assurne.

12 The thirteenth-century author of a *Continuation* to *Perceval* by Chrétien de Troyes.

13 An important Celtic deity, the son of the mother goddess Dôn, and brother of the likes of the goddess Arianrhod and the magician Gwydion fab Dôn.

14 King Arthur's mother following the magical transformation by Merlin of Uther into the exact likeness of her husband, Gorlois, Duke of Cornwall, the sworn enemy of Uther.

15 The most famous of all semi-legendary Welsh poets, his birth is covered in the profile for Sir Morfran ab Tegid (see pages 139–41).

16 The spear with which the centurion Gaius Cassius, later known as Longinus ('spearman') after his conversion to Christianity, was said to have pierced the side of Jesus Christ while the latter hung on the cross (St. John 19:xxxiv). The spear originally belonged to King Herod and was carried by Longinus as a symbol of his authority. It had, at least according to Judaic records, been forged under the direction of the ancient prophet Phineas. Some accounts say that it was also the spear that King Saul threw at the young David.

17 A historical king of the Brythonic kingdom of Rheged in northwest England, he reigned from *c.*570 to *c.*590, when he was assassinated by an ally following his defeat of the Bernicians, the inhabitants of a realm in the northeast.

18 Ancient Greek and Roman term for an Arab. During the Middle Ages it was used by Europeans to refer to all Muslims,

though the Spanish favoured the term Moor.

19 The daughter of Prester John, a legendary monarch thought to have ruled in either Africa or Asia.

King Arthur

1 This work purports to give an account of British history from the time of Julius Caesar to towards the end of the seventh century. It gives a mythical account of the origins of the British people and recounts the Roman occupation, the settlement of the Saxon invaders and King Arthur's 12 victories. Although the book contains fanciful material of doubtful historical significance, its real value lies in its preservation of material needed for the study of early Celtic literature in general, and the Arthurian legends in particular.

2 The 12 battles are listed by Nennius as: 1. at the mouth of the River Glein; 2–5. the River Douglas in Linnius (see note 7); 6. on the River Bassus; 7. at Cat Coit Celidon (Scotland or Lincolnshire); 8. at Guinnion; 9. at the City of the Legions (Caerleon-on-Usk or Chester); 10. at the River Tribuit; 11. at Mount Agned (possibly Rochester in Kent); 12. Mount Badon.

3 Pendragon is a title rather than a surname. It comes from the amalgamation of the Brythonic *pen* signifying 'head' or 'main', and the Old Welsh *dragawn* meaning leader. The title was taken by both Uther and his son, though it is normally applied only to Uther. It simply signifies that the holder of the title is the chief leader – a king.

4 The traditional home of Duke Gorlois which, due to its location, is totally inaccessible except by invitation, or by guile, a point relevant to the magical conception of King Arthur. At the time

when the romances were being written, the promontory on which the castle (now ruined) stands was connected to the mainland by a ridge that has since crumbled away. However, the present castle did not exist during the traditional period, for the ruins of the castle that are there today are those of the building that was started *c.*1141 by Reginald, Earl of Cornwall. Tintagel, it has been suggested, means 'almost an island'.

5 Anonymous thirteenth-century collection of prose romances that consists of the *Prose Lancelot*, the *Queste del Sainte Graal* and its prelude, the *Estoire del Sainte Graal*, the *Mort Artu*, the *Vulgate Merlin* and the *Vulgate Merlin Continuation*.

6 While no one has ever accurately derived the true meaning of the name Excalibur, some have sought to say that it means 'Cut Steel'. It is more likely to have derived from the magical sword Caladbolg, with which it can be linguistically linked, this latter sword (deriving its name from *calad*, 'hard', and *bolg*, 'lightning') was borne by Irish heroes, and in particular Cú Chulainn.

7 The scene of four of the battles fought by Arthur as listed by Nennius. The exact location has never been accurately determined, but it is now thought that Linnius might signify Lindsey, a region of modern-day Lincolnshire, a county with which Arthur has a number of associations.

8 Presumably not the same Lot who was originally an enemy of Arthur and the husband of Arthur's half-sister Morgause.

9 Described as the Lord of Moray (Scotland) and the father of Yvain (see profile, pages 156–9, though the latter is usually said to be the son of Urien of Rheged. This has led to some to say that Urian is simply a misspelling, but some sources do mention Urian quite independently of Urien.

10 King of Scotland according to Geoffrey of Monmouth, the brother of Urian and sometimes also of Lot. A staunch ally of Arthur, he accompanied the king on his campaign against the Roman Empire, but was killed at the battle of Richborough by Mordred.

11 Other contenders are Winchester, Caerleon-on-Usk and Colchester. The romances said that Camelot was named after a pagan king, Camaalis. Camelot first appears in the works of Chrétien de Troyes.

12 Both Wace and Sir Thomas Malory emphatically refer to Lucius Hiberius as 'emperor', though Geoffrey of Monmouth calls him *procurator* (governor), and thus implies that he was inferior to Leo, the Emperor of Constantinople.

13 The 12 who lay in wait to capture the adulterous Sir Lancelot are not all named, but those who specifically are were Agravain, Colgrevance, Daniel, Florence, Gareth, Lovel and Mordred.

14 The name given to England in the romances. It derives from Lloegr, the Old Welsh for England. Alternatively, it may have come from *legor*, an Anglo-Saxon element found in the place-name of Leicester.

15 The appearance of the Tower of London in this story is an anachronism. The keep, or White Tower, was not built until *c.*1078 by Bishop Gundulf, though it does stand on the site of earlier Roman and British fortifications, so it is quite possible that Guinevere could have barricaded herself into an earlier structure. The site is possibly most famous as being the legendary burial place of the head of Bendigeid Vran, the face forever turned towards France, which was intended to

serve as a guardian over Britain. Arthur was said to have dug up the head, for he alone wanted to be the guardian of his realm, a mistake that probably gave Mordred free reign.

16 There are many, many different locations ascribed to the battle of Camlann, including Salisbury Plain (Sir Thomas Malory), Ireland (the *Didot Perceval*), Cambridge and even the Roman fort of Camboglana on Hadrian's Wall. In fact, it has been mooted that just about anywhere with 'Cam' in its name could be considered a worthy contender – for example, Camulodunum, the Roman name for Colchester. There is just as much confusion over when the battle was fought. The *Annales Cambriae* state that it was fought 21 years after Badon, but as the dates used within this work are ambiguous, to say the least, this gives a span from 515 to 539. Geoffrey of Monmouth states that the battle was fought in 542, the Irish *Annals of Tigernach* give 541, while the Spanish *Annales Toledanos* place it as late as 580.

17 As with just about everything else to do with the Arthurian legends, there are many locations for the returning of Excalibur to the Lady of the Lake. The forerunner appears to be Dozmary Pool on Bodmin Moor, about 10 kilometres (6 miles) from Slaughterbridge. This would appear to tie in with the tradition of locating Camlann at Slaughterbridge, but the distance is all wrong, as the lake was said to be beside the battlefield and not some distance from it. Perhaps, the dying Arthur was carried the 10 kilometres before instructing Bedivere to follow his command. This would, of course, also make Dozmary Pool the lake across which the barge from Avalon came to carry the wounded king away to that fairy realm.

Sir Bedivere

1 The epithet *gafaelfawr* means 'great grasp' and was usually applied to Glewlwyd in his role as Arthur's porter (see page 49).

2 Numerous locations are suggested for this act, the most favoured being Dozmary Pool on Bodmin Moor, some 10 kilometres (6 miles) from Slaughterbridge, the traditional Cornish location for the battle of Camlann. This, however, does not take into account the fact that the battle was traditionally said to have been fought close to the lake and not some distance away. This is yet one more of the many confusions to be found throughout the Arthurian legends.

The Black Knight

1 The dual aspects found in the story of Cerridwen and her children are common to many mythologies and religions worldwide, being perhaps best illustrated in the eternal struggle between God and the devil.

2 An unidentified kingdom or race of people who appear only in Irish romances.

Sir Bors

1 The King of the Desert Land, who seized the kingdom of the elder Bors after his death. His realm has been identified with Berry, since *berrie* in Old French signifies a desert.

2 This is obviously a reworking of a much earlier pagan belief. Compare for example the shape-changing fury Cerridwen went through in her pursuit of the young Gwion Bach (see profile for Sir Morfran ab Tegid, pages 139–41).

3 Possibly a region of east Wales.

4 The father of Elaine and thus the grandfather of Sir Galahad (see profile,

pages 87–91). Pelles is just one of the many characters referred to in the legends that surround the quest for the Holy Grail as the Fisher King. Pelles was the son of Pellam, who had been struck the Dolorous Stroke by Sir Balin, and is called the King of Listinoise, though that realm is also ascribed to Pellehan, another of the many characters to be called the Fisher King. After the Dolorous Stroke had lain waste the realm, his kingdom became known as the Waste Land, though Pelles is sometimes called the King of Terre Foraine ('the Foreign Land').

Sir Galahad

1 A part of the French *Vulgate Version*, this section is thought to have been written by a Cistercian monk.

2 Christian festival occurring on Whit Sunday that commemorates the descent of the Holy Ghost on the Apostles. In Judaism it is the Jewish harvest festival that falls on the fiftieth day after the second day of the Passover.

3 So called because any who dared sit upon it, save that person for whom it was reserved, would be burnt to ashes for their presumption.

4 A king born in France, Evelake was sent to Rome as part of a tribute but escaped and travelled to Syria. There he killed the son of the governor and had to flee to Babylon, where he helped the king and was rewarded with land. Evelake became the King of Sarras (a pagan city often mentioned in the Grail legends), where he was baptized by Joseph of Arimathea, generally believed to be Jesus's uncle, and took the name Mordrain. His association with the Grail legends goes much further than his kingship of Sarras, for it is said that he lived with unhealing wounds and was sustained only by the

Holy Grail and would remain that way until the Holy Grail had been achieved by one of the questing knights.

5 Known as Agrestizia in Italian romance.

6 This sword is also sometimes referred to as the Sword of the Strange Hangings. Solomon, the son of King David, had placed it aboard his ship, unsurprisingly known as Solomon's ship in the legends, where it hung in hempen hangings made by Solomon's wife. After her death the hangings were said to have been replaced with some made from the hair of Dindrane, though this appears to be a relatively late development, for her hair, in this instance, was not used until after she had died, and therefore could not have been taken by Sir Galahad while she was still alive and travelling with the three knights.

7 Estorause was a successor to Evelake (see note 4), who obviously left the pagan city of Sarras following his conversion to Christianity. The exact location of the city of Sarras remains a mystery. Some sources place it in the vicinity of Jerusalem, a location obviously chosen during the Crusades; others in Britain itself. Little is known about the city apart from its pagan status – the Roman god Mars was worshipped there – though some sources state that the Saracens took their name from the city. However, the term Saracen was an ancient Greek and Roman one for an Arab and was in use long before the advent of the Grail legends.

Sir Gareth

1 Christian festival that lasts for the week that starts with Whit Sunday, the seventh Sunday after Easter, the first three days of the week being especially relevant. Whit

Sunday is actually another name for the feast of Pentecost, which celebrates the descent of the Holy Spirit on the Apostles.

2 This is not the same Green Knight as the one who challenged the Knights of the Round Table to the beheading game that only Sir Gawain was brave enough to take part in. That Green Knight was Sir Bertilak de Hautdesert, while this Green Knight is Sir Pertelope.

3 This trait of strength increasing in the morning and decreasing after midday is quite common within the Arthurian cycle. Gawain is said to possess this ability, as is one of that knight's enemies, Escanor. It appears to owe its origins to the Old Welsh character of Gwalchmai fab Gwyar whom some sources name as the origin of Sir Gawain.

4 Christian festival commemorating the taking up of the body and soul of the Virgin Mary into heaven after her days on earth had come to an end.

5 The feast of St Michael the Archangel, 29 September, and one of the four quarter days in England, Ireland and Wales.

Sir Gawain

1 In this story Arthur appears as the King of Ireland who married a mysterious woman who was brought to him on a bier, but then had to fight a man whom the king took to be the woman's lover. Arthur was defeated, but the man was then killed by Uallabh. It turned out that the man was the son of the King and brother of the Queen of Ineen who had imprisoned Uallabh, but had been set free by the queen's younger sister, whom he subsequently married and succeeded Arthur as the King of Ireland.

2 A purely fictitious character who is perhaps to be identified with Pope Simplicius (468–483).

3 This Italian working of the legends is, in fact, a version of the story of Lanval (see profile, pages 123–5). In it Pulzella Gaia becomes the mistress of Gawain and elicits from him a promise to keep their relationship secret. Gawain subsequently rebuffed the advances of Guinevere, who accused him of attempting to seduce her. He replied that he already loved another but could not reveal her identity as he had promised not to. She arrived in the nick of time, but was imprisoned by Morgan Le Fay, who made her stand in water up to her waist. Gawain rescued and married her, and imprisoned Morgan Le Fay.

Sir Kay

1 The position of seneschal was the most important of a number of household offices within a great medieval household. In a king's household, all these positions, such as butler, cupbearer, marshal, etc., would be held by nobles or knights of the realm.

Sir Lancelot

1 *Spoils of Annwfn*, allegedly written by Taliesin, this Welsh poem, which dates from *c*.900, describes the journey undertaken by Arthur and his companions to obtain an enchanted cauldron from the Otherworld, the story, and more centrally the cauldron, being considered as one of the various origins of the later Grail legends.

2 As Lancelot is universally regarded as having been raised by the Lady of the Lake, her realm often being referred to as Maidenland, some authorities have equated this fairy realm with the Irish Tír inna mBan, the Otherworld realm that is

otherwise referred to as the Land of Women. It is not hard to see how the connection has been made.

3 Astolat may come from Alclud, the old name for Dumbarton, through the intermediate form of Asclut, though Sir Thomas Malory places Astolat at Guildford in Surrey. Astolat is also known as Shalott, which explains why Elaine is known as the Lady of Shalott – also the title of the famous poem by Alfred, Lord Tennyson.

4 This part of the story would seem to confirm the location of Astolat at Guildford, for there is no way the body of Elaine could have been floated down the Thames from Dumbarton, no matter how far fetched the legends might have been.

5 As we have already seen, this is an anachronism for the Tower of London as it stands today was not built until approximately 500 years after the traditional Arthurian period, though the reference here might be to an earlier Roman or British fort that stood on the same site.

Sir Lanval

1 The story of Lanval was to resurface later in Italian romance, though this time it was Gawain who had a fairy lover and fell foul of the adulterous attentions of Guinevere. In this version the fairy maiden is called Pulzella Gaia ('Cheerful Damsel'), and is the daughter of Morgan Le Fay. Pulzella Gaia warned Gawain to keep their romance a secret, a promise he broke when he rebuffed Guinevere. As with Lanval, so with Gawain: the maiden appeared at the eleventh hour, but she warned Gawain that her mother would now imprison her, which she did, forcing her daughter to stand in water to her waist. Gawain then

came to the aid of Pulzella Gaia, freed her and imprisoned Morgan Le Fay.

Merlin

1 Published 1622 but written some time earlier. Although anonymous, it has been suggested that the play may have been written by W. Rowley (d. 1626), while its style suggests that William Shakespeare (1564–1616) may have had a hand in it.

2 Vortigern is now generally regarded as a historical character. Nennius places the start of his reign in 425. His name appears to mean 'overlord' and may, therefore, have simply been a title. He became king after having King Constantine, the grandfather of King Arthur, murdered, followed by that king's son Constans after which he usurped the throne himself with Pictish help. He then joined forces with the Saxons Hengist and Horsa in order to repel the Picts, and subsequently abdicated in favour of his son Vortimer. When Vortimer was poisoned by his stepmother, Vortigern once again became king. He fled to Wales after the slaughter of the British princes by Hengist on Salisbury Plain, and it was here that he came into contact with Merlin.

3 A wooded hill approximately 3 kilometres (2 miles) northeast of Beddgelert, Gwynedd, north Wales. There are still some earthworks of an ancient fort to be seen on the hill. Traces of a ruined tower some 11 by 7 metres (36 by 24 feet) have been found on the summit.

4 The son of King Constantine and brother of Uther and Constans, thus the uncle of Arthur. Of undoubted historicity, Ambrosius Aurelius was smuggled to Brittany after the death of Constans. Returning some years later with Uther, he defeated Vortigern and then went on to defeat the Saxons and had Hengist

executed. He was killed by Paschent, one of Vortigern's sons.

5 Every May Day Eve a scream was heard, the source of which could not be located. Llefelys, the King of France and brother of Llud, advised that the scream was caused by two fighting dragons, one red and one white. These were trapped in a pit in the centre of the country (Oxford) and subsequently interred beneath Dinas Emrys.

6 Properly known in Welsh as Arfderydd, this battle was fought *c.*575 for a 'lark's nest', which seems to indicate that the battle was over ownership of the important harbour of Caerlaverlock – 'Fort Lark'.

7 Welsh sources, who name Merlin's sister as Gwendydd, know nothing of this relationship. It is only in the *Vita Merlini* of Geoffrey of Monmouth that she appears as the unfaithful wife of Rhydderch Hael.

8 Possibly to be identified with Blodeuwedd, the flower maiden of Welsh mythology, Guendoloena, who has also been assimilated with Chwimleian, who appears in the Welsh Myrddin poem *Afollonau*, is thought by some to be the forerunner of the unfortunate Queen Guinevere.

9 The Hohenstaufen were a German princely family that provided rulers of Germany (1138–1208, 1214–54), Sicily (1194–1268) and the Holy Roman Empire (1138–1254). They were the first German emperors to make use of associations with Roman law to aggrandize their office. Their most famous emperor was Barbarossa (Frederick I) who was the first to use the title Holy Roman Emperor. The last of the line, Conradin, was executed in 1268, with the approval of Pope Clement IV, while attempting to gain his Sicilian inheritance.

10 Italian family who were rulers of Ferrara between 1000 and 1875.

11 King of the Huns from 434 and called by some the 'Scourge of God'. He embarked on a vast range of conquests from the Rhine to Persia. He invaded Gaul in 451, but was defeated by the Roman and Visigothic armies under Aëtius and Theodoric I. In 452 he entered Italy and was stopped from sacking Rome only by the intervention of Pope Leo I. He died on the night of his marriage to Ildico, possibly being poisoned, and is alleged to have been buried with a vast treasure.

12 Called Ynys Enlli in Welsh, this small island lies just off the tip of the Lleyn peninsula in Gwynedd, at the northern entrance of Cardigan Bay. Now a bird sanctuary and observatory, the island was an important holy site to the Celts, who built a monastery, now ruined, there in the sixth century. The island has become known as the Island of the Twenty Thousand Saints, for that number of Celtic saints are alleged to be buried there.

Sir Mordred

1 As we have already seen, this is an anachronism, for the Tower of London as it stands today was not built until approximately 500 years after the traditional Arthurian period, though the reference here might be to an earlier Roman or British fort that stood on the same site.

2 The relevant entry reads: 'Year 93: the strife of Camlann in which Arthur and Medrawt perished; and there was plague in Britain and Ireland.' Some authorities have sought to make Year 93 mean 538, by placing Year 1 at 445, but there is no way of actually calculating the date meant by either Year 1 or Year 93. The *Annales*

Cambriae are notoriously unreliable for dates, but may prove the existence of both Arthur and Mordred, as everyone else mentioned there was real.

Sir Morfran ab Tegid

1 Identified as one of the possible origins of the Holy Grail. The use of the cauldron in the story of Cerridwen and her magical conception embodies many spiritual principles that are as relevant to the Christian Grail as they are to the pagan cauldron of the Otherworld.

2 The Welsh name for Virgil (70–19 BC), the great Roman poet who possibly owes his position within this story to the Roman occupation of Wales.

3 The father of Elphin and the owner of a prolific salmon weir, the fish presumably being poisoned in the same manner as his horses. Gwyddno Garanhir is considered historical, a prince or king of Gwynedd. He was also said to have owned a *mwys*, or basket, which could feed 100 people at a time, an object that Merlin (see profile, pages 127–33) took with him as one of the Thirteen Treasures of Britain, and that, like the cauldron of Cerridwen, seems to recall the earlier memories of the magical cauldron of the Otherworld.

4 A monstrous, mythical member of the cat family. The Welsh poem *Pa gur* tells how Sir Kay travelled to Anglesey with a view to killing lions, but especially prepared for a meeting with the Cath Palug. *Palug* means 'clawing'. Some authorities have claimed that a leopard, kept as a pet by a Welsh king and having escaped from its owner, may have given rise to this legend.

5 Described as a region within Annwfn, the Welsh Otherworld, where there flowed a fountain of wine, and no one ever knew illness or old age. The variant of Caer Rigor seems to suggest a realm from which there is no return, even though on one occasion the land was visited by King Arthur and his retinue.

6 Neoloithic is derived from two Greek words: *neo*, 'new', and *lithos* 'a stone'. The Neolithic age was the last period of the Stone Age during which time people progressed to making the first steps in agriculture, domestication of animals, weaving and pottery making. The Celts originated during this period.

Sir Perceval

1 The Grail procession appears in works only when it is Sir Perceval rather than Sir Galahad who achieves the Holy Grail. According to Chrétien de Troyes, the Grail was carried in a procession led by a squire holding a bleeding lance (presumably the Lance of Longinus). He was followed by two squires carrying ten branched candlesticks, a damsel carrying the Grail itself and a final damsel carrying a plate. There are various other descriptions of the procession. The French *Didot Perceval* described the order of the procession as a squire with a lance, a damsel with two plates and cloths, and finally a squire with a vessel (the Grail) containing the blood of Christ. The Welsh *Peredur* says that the procession consisted of two youths carrying a large spear from which blood flowed freely, followed by a damsel carrying a salver on which there was a head swimming in blood.

2 The question required to break the enchantment under with the Fisher King and all his lands were held. The question is really two: 'What is the Grail?' and 'Whom does it serve?'

3 Trebuchet appears to owe his origins to Turbe, the father of the Irish smith god Goibhniu.

4 Title given to the descendants of Joseph of Arimathea, Jesus's uncle, who guarded the Holy Grail.

5 A French prose romance that dates from *c.*1200. Although it is anonymous, it has been suggested that the work was by Robert de Boron.

6 A mythical Welsh monster whose name, in modern Welsh, means 'beaver'.

7 Thirteenth-century French romance that forms a part of the *Vulgate Version* that introduces Sir Galahad as the successful quester. It is thought to have been written by a Cistercian monk.

8 Usually identified as north Wales, which would indicate that Herzeloyde was the queen of all Wales. Northgalis has also sometimes been identified with a north Briton realm, perhaps Strathclyde, with which Wales was closely allied.

Sir Tristan

1 Said to have been born in Gaul, Gorvenal later served as Tristan's servant and married Brangien, Iseult's handmaiden. He ascended the throne of Liones after Tristan had departed.

2 A great deal of confusion surrounds this character, who is also called Marhalt. He was, according to Sir Thomas Malory, the King of Ireland and father of Marhaus, the latter being elsewhere known simply as Morholt's ally. Marhaus is also known as Moraunt. The chronology of Morholt is particularly confused, for when he fought Tristan he was said to have been the brother-in-law of the then king, Anguish, and did not himself ascend the throne until some time later, something that would have been impossible as Tristan had

already killed him. However, it is usually thought that Tristan in fact fought his son Marhaus, and thus left Morholt alive to become king later. The picture is extremely unclear and regrettably, as with so much else in the Arthurian cycle, it is impossible to untangle the confusion left by the early writers.

3 Yet more confusion ensues, as Iseult is here said to be the daughter of Anguish, but she is earlier said to have been the daughter of Morholt. It now seems likely that Iseult was originally married to Marhaus, making Anguish her father-in-law, and that Anguish agreed to the marriage between Iseult and Mark after Tristan had killed Iseult's husband in the earlier combat.

4 There is no conclusive identity for the Duchy of Swales, though some commentators have sought to make the simple, though dubious, assumption that it is cognate with south Wales ('S. Wales = Swales').

5 The cousin, or possibly nephew, of King Arthur who helped the young king at the start of his reign to put down the rebellion of the 11 barons opposed to the kingship passing to a 15-year-old boy.

6 A theme possibly taken from classical Greek mythology, where Theseus, the son of Aegeus King of Athens, promises that the ship taking him to Crete to do battle with the Minotaur will return with white sails if he has been successful and black ones if he has died. Theseus killed the Minotaur but forgot to hoist the white sails. When his father saw the black sails, he threw himself from the Acropolis into the sea, which has from that day been known as the Aegean Sea.

7 Gráinne was the beautiful daughter of Cormac mac Airt who was betrothed to the ageing Fionn mac Cumhaill. She fell in

love with Diarmaid ua Duibhne and forced him to elope with her. Fionn mac Cumhaill laid siege to them, but later became reconciled with the couple. However, during the hunt for the great boar Beann Ghulban, Diarmaid ua Duibhne was fatally gored and only water from the hands of Fionn mac Cumhaill could save his life. Three times Fionn mac Cumhaill went to fetch water, but each he time let it slip through his fingers as he remembered the treachery of Gráinne and Diarmaid ua Duibhne. By the time he returned for the third time, Diarmaid ua Duibhne was dead.

8 An historical ruler of ancient Cornwall and Brittany, who, according to legend, attempted to save himself from being killed by one of his offspring as had been prophesied by killing all his wives when they became pregnant. One, Trephina, managed to evade him until after she had given birth. She was subsequently beheaded but, restored to life, she picked up her head and went back to Cunomorus's castle, where the battlements promptly fell on Cunomorus and killed him.

Sir Yvain

1 The great mother goddess, whose name simply means 'mother'. She is the early Welsh equivalent of the classical Roman goddess Matrona.

2 Also known as Le chevalier au lion – 'The Knight of the Lion'.

3 Situated in Brittany and today known as the Forest of Paimpont. The forest was the setting for a number of Arthurian adventures, possibly none more potent than that recounted by the French poet Huon de Mery in his *Le tornoiment de l'Antichrist*. In this he explains how he travelled to an enchanted spring in the forest where he was approached by Bras-de-Fer, chamberlain of the Antichrist, who took him to the scene of a great battle in which the forces of hell were battling against the forces of heaven, which included King Arthur and his knights.

Further Reading

Ashe, G. *The Discovery of King Arthur* Guild, London, 1985

Barber, R. *The Arthurian Legends* The Boydell Press, Woodbridge, Suffolk, 1979

Béroul *The Romance of Tristan* (trans. A. S. Fredrick) Penguin Books, Harmondsworth, 1970

Bogdanow, F. *The Romances of the Grail* Manchester University Press, Manchester, 1966

Brengle, R. L. (ed.) *Arthur King of Britain* Appleton–Century–Crofts, New York, 1964

Briel, H. and Herrmann, M. *King Arthur's Knights and the Myths of the Round Table* Klincksieck, Paris, 1972

Brodeur, A. G. *Arthur Dux Bellorum* University of California Press, Berkeley, 1939

Brown, A. C. L. *The Origin of the Grail Legend* Harvard University Press, Cambridge, Mass., 1943

Bruce, J. D. *The Evolution of Arthurian Romance* P. Smith, Gloucester, Mass., 1958

Cavendish, R. *King Arthur and the Grail* Weidenfeld & Nicolson, London, 1978

Chrétien de Troyes *Arthurian Romances* (trans. N. Briant) Dent, London, 1955

—*Perceval* (trans. N. Briant) Boydell & Brewer, Cambridge, 1982

Coghlan, R. *The Encyclopaedia of Arthurian Legends* Element Books, Shaftesbury, 1991

Davis, C. *King Arthur's Return* Blandford, London, 1995

Day, M. L. *De Ortu Waluuanii* translated as *The Rise of Gawain* Garland Press, New York, 1984

Didot Perceval translated as *The Romance of Perceval in Prose* University of Washington Press, Seattle, 1966

Ditmas, E. M. R. *Tristan and Iseult in Cornwall* Forrester Roberts, Gloucester, 1969

Dixon-Kennedy, M. *Arthurian Myth & Legend: An A–Z of People and Places* Blandford, London, 1995

— *Celtic Myth & Legend: An A–Z of People and Places* Blandford, London, 1996

Eisner, S. *The Tristan Legend* Northwestern University Press, Evanston, 1969

Fedrick, A. S. (trans.) *'The Romance of Tristan' by Beroul and 'The Tale of Tristan's Madness'* Penguin Books, Harmondsworth, Middlesex, 1970

Gantz, J. (trans.) *The Mabinogion* Penguin Books, Harmondsworth, 1976

Geoffrey of Monmouth *History of the Kings of Britain* (trans. L. Thorpe) Penguin Books, Harmondsworth, Middlesex, 1966

—*Vita Merlini* (trans. J. J. Parry) University of Illinois Press, Urbana, 1925

Goodrich, N. L. *King Arthur* Watts, Danbury, 1986

Gottfried von Strassburg *Tristan* (trans. A. T. Hatto) Penguin Books, Harmondsworth, Middlesex, 1960

Guest, Lady Charlotte. (trans.) *The Mabinogion* J. Jones, Cardiff, 1977

Holmes, U. T. and Klenke, M. A. *Chrétien de Troyes and the Grail* University of North Carolina Press, Chapel Hill, 1959

Hopkins, A. *Chronicles of King Arthur* Collins & Brown Ltd., London, 1993

Jarman, A. O. H. *The Legend of Merlin* University of Wales Press, Cardiff, 1960

Jones, G. and Jones, T. (trans.) *The Mabinogion* Dent, London, 1949

Jung, E. and von Franz, M. L. *The Grail Legend* Hodder & Stoughton, London, 1972

Knight, G. *The Secret Tradition in the Arthurian Legend* Aquarian Press, Wellingborough, 1984

Lacy, N. J. (ed.) *The Arthurian Encyclopedia*, Garland Press, New York, 1986

* Lawhead, S. *Taliesin: Book I of the Pendragon Cycle* Lion Publishing, Oxford, 1988

— *Merlin: Book II of the Pendragon Cycle* Lion Publishing, Oxford, 1988.

— *Arthur: Book III of the Pendragon Cycle* Lion Publishing, Oxford, 1989

Loomis, R. S. *Arthurian Tradition and Chrétien de Troyes* Columbia University Press, New York, 1949

— *The Grail: From Celtic Myth to Christian Symbol* University of Wales Press, Cardiff, 1963

— *'The Romance of Tristram and Ysolt' by Thomas of Britain* Columbia University Press, New York, 1951

— *Arthurian Literature in the Middle Ages* Clarendon Press, Oxford, 1959

Luttrell, C. *The Creation of the First Arthurian Romance*, London, 1974

Malory, Sir Thomas, *Le Morte d'Arthur* Penguin Books, Harmondsworth, Middlesex, 1969

Marie de France (trans. E. Mason) *Lays* Dent, London, 1955

Markale, J. *King Arthur: King of Kings* Gordon & Cremonesi, London, 1977

Matarasso, P. M. (trans.) *The Quest of the Holy Grail (Quest Sainte Graal)* Penguin Books, Harmondsworth, Middlesex, 1969

Matthews, John *The Grail* Thames & Hudson, London, 1981

—*The Elements of the Arthurian Tradition* Element, Shaftesbury, 1989

— *The Elements of the Grail Tradition* Element, Shaftesbury, 1990

— *Gawain: Knight of the Goddess* Aquarian Press, Wellingborough, 1990

— *King Arthur and the Grail Quest* Blandford, London, 1994

Matthews, J. and Stewart, R. J. *Warriors of Arthur* Blandford, London, 1987

Michell, J.   *The Travellers Key to Sacred England: A Guide to the Legends, Lore, and Landscape of England's Sacred Places*   Harrap Columbus, London, 1989

Moorman, C. and Moorman, R.   *An Arthurian Dictionary*   University of Mississippi Press, Jackson, 1978

Morris, J.   *The Age of Arthur*   Weidenfeld & Nicolson, London, 1973

Owen, D. D. R.   *The Evolution of the Grail Legend*   Oliver & Boyd, Edinburgh, 1968

Saklatvala, B.   *Arthur: Roman Britain's Last Champion*   David & Charles, Newton Abbot, 1967

Sommer, H. O. (ed.)   *Vulgate Version*   Carnegie Institution, Washington, 1908–16

Stewart, R. J.   *The Prophetic Vision of Merlin*   Arkana, London, 1985 (ed.)

— *The Mystic Life of Merlin*   Arkana, London, 1986

— *The Book of Merlin*   Blandford, Poole, 1987

— *Celtic Gods, Celtic Goddesses*   Blandford, London, 1990

— *Celtic Myths, Celtic Legends*   Blandford, London, 1994

Stewart, R. J. and Matthews, J.   *Merlin Through the Ages*   Blandford, London, 1995

Stone, B. (trans.)   *Sir Gawain and the Green Knight*   Penguin Books, Harmondsworth, Middlesex, 1959

Stuart–Knill, Sir Ian   *The Pedigree of Arthur*   Kingdom Revival Crusade, Sidmouth, 1977

Tolkien, J. R. R. and Gordon, E. V. (eds.)   *Sir Gawain and the Green Knight* (2nd edition revised by N. Davis), Clarendon Press, Oxford, 1967

Tolstoy, N.   *The Quest for Merlin*   Hamish Hamilton, London, 1985

Ulrich von Zatzikhoven   *Lancelot* (trans. K. G. T. Webster)   Columbia University Press, New York, 1951

Vinaver, E. (ed.)   *The Works of Sir Thomas Malory* (3 vols.)   The Clarendon Press, Oxford, 1947

Wace and Layamon   *Arthurian Chronicles*   Dent, London, 1962

Weston, J. L.   (trans.) *'Parzival', A Knightly Epic by Wolfram von Eschenbach*   David Nutt, London, 1894

— *The Legend of Sir Gawain*   David Nutt, London, 1897

Wirnt von Grafenberg   *Wigalois* (trans. J. W. Thomas)   University of Nebraska Press, Lincoln (Nebraska), 1977

Wolfram von Eschenbach   *Parzival* (trans. A. T. Hatto)   Penguin Books, Harmondsworth, 1980

* The three books listed above by Stephen Lawhead are fiction, but they are worthy of attention as they draw heavily on the Arthurian legends and give a modern interpretation of them.

Index